Your College Years

Your College Years

Secrets of the Universe to Make Them the Best

Catherine DePino

ROWMAN & LITTLEFIELD
Lanham • Boulder • New York • London

Published by Rowman & Littlefield
An imprint of The Rowman & Littlefield Publishing Group, Inc.
4501 Forbes Boulevard, Suite 200, Lanham, Maryland 20706
www.rowman.com

86-90 Paul Street, London EC2A 4NE, United Kingdom

British Library Cataloguing in Publication Information Available

Library of Congress Cataloging-in-Publication Data

Names: DePino, Catherine, author.
Title: Your college years : secrets of the universe to make them the best
    / Catherine DePino.
Description: Lanham, Maryland : Rowman & Littlefield, [2022] |
    Summary: "Your College Years deals with topics that help students
    know how to handle situations they'll encounter during their college
    years"— Provided by publisher.
Identifiers: LCCN 2021061696 (print) | LCCN 2021061697 (ebook)
    | ISBN 9781475863383 (Paperback : acid-free paper) | ISBN
    9781475863390 (ePub)
Subjects: LCSH: College student orientation—United States. | College
    students—United States—Social conditions. | College students—
    United States—Life skills guides.
Classification: LCC LB2343.32 .D38 2022 (print) | LCC LB2343.32
    (ebook) | DDC 378.1/980973—dc23/eng/20220110
LC record available at https://lccn.loc.gov/2021061696
LC ebook record available at https://lccn.loc.gov/2021061697

♾️™ The paper used in this publication meets the minimum requirements of
American National Standard for Information Sciences—Permanence of Paper for
Printed Library Materials, ANSI/NISO Z39.48-1992.

To my dear granddaughter, Hope Caterina Kudgis

"Shall I compare thee to a summer's day?
Thou art more lovely and more temperate . . ."
—*William Shakespeare*

Contents

Reader's Note

"Dear Incoming Students: You are about to embark on an experience that will remain embossed on your mind for the remainder of your life. You will be challenged intellectually, your character will be tested, perseverance tried, and emotions plumbed. The significance of this endeavor is recognized by society, which is why on the other side, after graduation, you will no longer be a young adult, but welcomed as a full-fledged adult. University is not the only path there, but the best one, as exposure to the knowledge and wisdom of the world affects the mind, the character, and the soul. Good luck."—Lanny Larcinese, one who's been to college and succeeded

Preface

This book is for educators, counselors, and parents of prospective college students who want to help them succeed in college by having a superior academic and social experience. Teachers and counselors will want to buy the book from their allotments to accompany presentations about college that they conduct with individuals and small and large groups. Parents, family members, and friends will want to buy the book for high school students intent on succeeding in college and beyond.

At the same time, *Your College Years* is also directed to students who hope to learn about what their college experience will be like and who are looking for ways to succeed throughout their college years. Parents, relatives, and friends can buy the book for high school and college students so that they can get a clear picture of the college experience in all its aspects.

Going from high school to college presents challenges even to the best and most well-adjusted students. Young people entering college need inside information about what it takes to get through college with a minimum of stress and want to learn how to navigate the system like pros. This book addresses the problems many students encounter during their freshman and subsequent years and offers them viable solutions to help them deal with the challenges they'll face.

Many college freshmen believe that they can pick up where they left off in high school and easily find friends and satisfaction taking their courses. Although some may adjust easily, most students find that it takes time and effort to learn how to balance college work, demanding professors, roommate problems, and testing situations they've never experienced in high school.

I wrote this book to help college students learn the ins and outs of college life and how to come out on top with a winning job waiting for them in the future.

My main goal in writing this book is to give educators, counselors, and parents a springboard for discussions about college's joys and challenges before they go to college. Students reading the book will hopefully enter college with their hearts and minds fully opened up about what to expect on this new and exciting journey. The practical and time-tested ideas in this book will send students to the head of the class and put them ahead of the game before their adventure begins.

Acknowledgments

Thanks to the following people who supplied questions and insights for chapter 11 and for the book as a whole: Jacquelyn Massott Campbell, Douglas Cooper, Dr. Andrew DePino, Lauren DePino, Gavin Hawk, Cole Kudgis, Shayna Kudgis, Lanny Larcinese, Joseph Spinelli, and Dr. Monica Uhlhorn.

Introduction

The book is organized in eleven chapters. All the chapters relate to helping prospective and current college students make the most of their college years and guiding them in finding the right path to their lifelong careers. Although the book can stand on its own as a practical guidebook for prospective college students, it is mainly intended as a resource for educators, teachers, and counselors to assist students desiring a successful college career.

Your College Years deals with topics that help students know how to handle situations they'll encounter during their college years. It addresses settling in and making new friends. It also deals with different types of college experiences, such as living on campus versus commuting.

An important feature of the book deals with knowing where to go for help when students need it, regarding academic or mental health issues. Moreover, the book suggests helpful solutions for coping with stress. Another important feature of this book relates to making the most of class time and managing time wisely so that students live a balanced life, which is vital for good mental and physical health.

If students want to learn how to excel in taking different types of tests, this book will help them. It explains how to take and excel in objective and essay tests. A highly effective and student-friendly outlining technique will help students write superior essays every time.

Your College Years also helps students choose a major and a minor in line with their passion and discusses the importance of networking in finding the perfect job.

Each chapter contains takeaways at the chapter's end so that students can review the content at a glance.

The final section of the book, "Questions and Answers about College" offers actual questions from parents and students and provides answers about how to experience the college years in the best possible way to ensure success.

This book targets itself to educators, counselors, and parents, in hopes that they will help students become well-prepared for college by following its principles. For this reason, I've included activities at the end of each chapter that school personnel can use with their students in individual, small, and large group settings.

Find these questions in the section labeled "Discuss" after the Takeaways. The activities easily lend themselves to English classes and guidance periods. Teachers can base reading, writing, and speaking activities on each of the chapter contents. Counselors will find the study guide helpful for helping students bridge the gap between high school and college. Parents can also use the questions as a springboard for creating their own discussion topics.

Chapter 1

Listen Up

Learn How to Play the Game

MESSAGE FROM THE DEAN

It's freshman orientation. You're sitting with a roomful of students in a stifling auditorium waiting to learn how to stay in college now that your top college pick accepted you. A bald man with a booming voice strides to the podium and waits for pin-drop silence.

"Welcome, ladies and gentleman. I'm Dr. James, Dean of Students. I want you to turn to the right." A roomful of heads turns to the right. The Dean ramps up his volume. "Now, I need you to turn to the left." All heads jerk to the left.

"Now face front," the Dean intones like a drill sergeant. The audience rearranges itself in narrow auditorium chairs, rushing to follow the Dean's command.

You wonder if this is boot camp and not the fun party school you happily anticipated. Why did you leave your loving home and cozy high school where you were voted prom king or queen or gym night captain to face this unhappy welcome at the hands of this ruthless drill sergeant?

The Dean lowers his voice. He reminds you of the picture you saw in your senior lit book of Jonathan Edwards delivering his fiery sermon, "Sinners in the Hands of an Angry God."

"Remember the faces you saw to the left and the right of you, and include your own. Make no mistake. Only one out of three in attendance here today will survive freshman year. When you feel like staying out all night at a frat party or skipping class because sleeping soothes your soul, don't give into your baser instincts. You may be one of the three who doesn't make it through this college. You'll be remembered as a college drop-out for the rest of your life. Listen to what we say today and listen well. Your future depends on it."

Without further ado, the dean assigns you to small groups, and a student orientation leader takes over.

PLATO, THE WISE

The orientation leader's horn-rimmed glasses perch over his owl nose, and red pimples splotch his pasty face. He reminds you of Rumpelstiltskin and carries a worn briefcase. A name tag on his university T-shirt reads, "Hi, I'm Plato."

You wonder if that's his first or last name. Could he be the illustrious philosopher reincarnated? More importantly, will he teach you the secrets of the universe guaranteed to ensure your academic and social success in college?

Plato shepherds you into an empty classroom. What he has to tell you will take only a few minutes, he says, and if everyone gives him their kind attention, he'll reveal how he managed to maintain a 4.0 average throughout college and become the president of the chess team and the debate club and the head orientation leader. "If you want to know how to ace your courses you've come to the right place," he says and hops up on the desk.

A guy in the last row, sporting a reversed baseball hat and a hoop earring shouts, "You probably study eight hours a day and live like a monk. I like to get good grades, but I also like to have fun. So do my friends here," he says, scanning the audience with his hand.The audience titters, and Plato gives them a knowing smile.

"You may not believe this, but I major in pre-med and have a hot girlfriend."

We gaze at him incredulously. Really?

"Tell us more," a girl in the front row calls out.

PSYCH OUT YOUR PROFESSORS

"It's easy to come out on top in college," Plato says, and you don't need advanced degrees to do it. All you need to do is psychoanalyze your professor.

"I'm not a psych major," the guy with the reversed baseball hat says. "I'm not Sigmund Freud. I'm a sports fitness guy. So, what's the deal, Plato?"

"It's not hard. Everyone here can do it. Here's the plan. When your teachers give their introductory speeches about course requirements in those crucial first weeks, listen to what they say and how they say it. I mean really listen. Check out their body language. Ask yourself if they appear rigid or flexible, open to new ideas, or set in their ways. Your first-hand observations will help you determine how to study for their classes and present answers in tests they'll view favorably. That means good grades for you."

A freckle-faced fellow in the back row raises his hand. "So, I understand the prof's requirements. I can understand them perfectly and still fail the course, right?"

"It's possible, but if you know how the teacher expects you to approach the subject, you'll have a better chance of acing the course. For example, if your professors stress the importance of notes they give in class to the exclusion of class discussion and textbook material, they're probably mainly interested in your concentrating on information they talk about in class.

"On the other hand, if a teacher encourages you to think critically and creatively, they'll welcome your point of view and thinking outside the box, in addition to parroting back the bare-boned facts. Alternatively, if the professor emphasizes the text, focus on mastering facts and dates when you study for exams. Pay attention to the chapter previews, dark print, and chapter summaries in the textbook. Quiz yourself on the review sections in the book.

"It always helps to let what the professor says during the opening days of class guide your decisions about how to study for the course so that you have a better chance of getting the grade you want.

"Knowing how to approach the teacher also helps when you don't understand the subject. Here's where a knowledge of body language comes in handy. Observe the way your teachers stand and move. Are they relaxed and laid back, or do they stand behind their desks with their arms folded? If they consistently stand, walk, or make eye contact in a certain way, you can draw conclusions about how approachable they are and how accepting they'll be if your ideas differ from theirs. The main word is *consistently*. If they don't act a certain way most the time, it's harder to draw conclusions about their psychological make-up, but you can still do it if you observe how they act most of the time.

"Ask yourself if the instructor appears rigid or open to new ideas, business-like or impersonal, or warm and friendly. You can get clues by the way they move and carry themselves. If they appear more open in the way they stand and move physically, they're more likely to listen to your views and not steadfastly promote and defend their own. If they look closed-off and resistant to your ideas with rigid body language and poor eye contact, they're likely to hold on to their own ideas rather than open themselves to yours.

"After you've tried to figure out your professors by studying their statements and body language, you'll know more about how to ask for help in a conference. If the teacher's approach is formal, try taking the same tone. Speak more formally than you would to a teacher who tells you to drop by the office to chat. This is part of rapport building and helps you communicate more effectively. No matter what your teacher's style, clarify with them what you don't understand and ask for specific suggestions that will help you get a better handle on the subject."

"I hear you, Plato," a long-haired girl in the front row says. "Now what can I do to make my teacher hear and remember me as an individual rather than as a nameless face in a huge lecture hall?"

Plato hops off the desk and stuffs his notes into his backpack. "Speak out in class early on. Ask questions. Seek clarification about what your teachers say. Make yourself known and stand out from the crowd.

"Make good eye contact with your teacher in a conference, but don't stare to make them uncomfortable. Try imitating their body language, but not in an obvious way, so they feel comfortable talking with you. Avoid overuse of your hands, and make your gestures smooth rather than forced and jerky when you talk to them.

"Ask if the teacher holds study groups or tutoring sessions and learn what additional texts or internet resources will help you get a better grasp of the subject. Your specific questions will help the teacher give you usable, concrete help in performing well in the course."

A bell blasts through the PA system. "Session's over. Just remember: to ace your courses, make a point to learn everything you can about your subjects, know your professors, and establish rapport with them from Day 1."

You walk out of the classroom into the late summer sun feeling as if you've learned the secrets of the universe. You run to catch up to Plato to thank him, but he's already trudging up the library stairs to meet another group of freshmen waiting to learn his secrets about how to succeed in college.

TAKEAWAYS

- Figure Out What Makes Your Professors Tick
- Know How Your Teacher Expects You to Approach the Subject
- Observe Your Professor's Body Language
- Pay Attention to What Teachers Say During First Days of Class about Course Requirements
- Stand Out from the Crowd: Make Your Teachers Notice You
- Always Ask When You Don't Understand Something
- Establish Rapport with Your Teachers from Day 1.

DISCUSS

- How can you figure out what makes your professors tick? How can you understand what they want from you so that you can get a good grade?
- Why is your teacher's body language important in interpreting their message? How can listening to what your teacher says and watching their body language help you understand how you should approach a testing situation?
- How can knowing about body language help you in a conference with your teacher?
- How can you make yourself stand out from the crowd so your teacher remembers you?

Chapter 2

Settle In

MAKE NEW FRIENDS BUT KEEP
THE OLD: STRIKE A BALANCE

Adjusting to college presents a new set of challenges, but with determination and ingenuity you can meet them. You're away from home, maybe for the first time. Even if you commute, you'll spend a lot of time in your new surroundings away from family and longtime friends. Strike a balance between staying in touch with old friends and making new ones. It helps to find students who live in your area so you can share rides home, and if you already know them, to reminisce about happy times in your neighborhood to get a sense of home while you're away.

It's also important to avoid making decisions based on your life before college. You may find yourself having to decide things well in advance, like spending a year abroad or working in an internship. In these cases, your current situation or your romantic relationships may enter into what you decide to do months from the time of an event, like an upcoming study opportunity. Case in point: Isabella came from a small Midwestern town to Temple, a large urban university in Philadelphia. In her senior year of high school, she found herself romantically involved with a pre-law college student from her hometown whom she eventually planned to marry.

In her freshman year, the Spanish department invited her to study abroad in Spain for her sophomore year. Naturally, she was torn about whether to be away from her boyfriend Colin for the whole year or to accept this opportunity of a lifetime, especially since she majored in world languages and planned to work as an interpreter for a government agency. When the time came to apply for the fellowship, Isabella opted for a less prestigious summer program in Spain instead of the more intensive year-long program that would afford her the chance for a graduate school scholarship. This would make it easier for her and Colin to see one another.

Later, she regretted making the decision to take the shorter program based on her relationship with Colin. Once she left for college and Colin became immersed in his pre-law studies and demanding internship, their relationship began to cool. Eventually, their year-long relationship came to an end because neither of them wanted to commit to a long-distance relationship.

Isabella's experience shows that it's important to make decisions related to your future by keeping in mind that your goals and circumstances may change once you enter college. It's better to base your plans on possibilities the future holds rather than rely on what your life looked like before you started college. There's always the chance that things may not turn out to be what you expected. Even though you hope your life will turn out a certain way, plan for different options because nothing in life is guaranteed, not even what appears to be the love of a lifetime.

FIND FRIENDS BY JOINING A CLUB

When Tomás, a student at Arizona State University, started college, he wanted to go home every weekend because he missed his friends and family. That required a long car ride that took time away from his studies. He became so homesick that he visited the counseling center, which advised him to join an organization to make new friends to occupy his free time, so he'd want to return home less often and would feel more comfortable in his new surroundings on campus.

Although he didn't enjoy being around people other than his family and friends, he decided to join the Newman Club, a faith-based club that sponsored weekend events, such as picnics, field trips, and shows. The club's president had spoken at the student activities segment of orientation, and he'd come across as a friendly guy who said the club would help people make friends in a homelike setting. As Tomás got to know more people from the club, he took advantage of their social activities and gradually experienced less desire to return home on weekends.

At around the same time, he met Shawna, a girl in his science class, who lived close to his old neighborhood, and they arranged to share rides home. Now, they're dating, and they're both spending more time on campus and less time missing their old high school connections.

Look for a group that complements your religion on campus. Many different faiths, such as Christian, Jewish, Muslim, and others sponsor organizations where students can take part in religious and social activities.

MAKE ROOM FOR NEW FRIENDS

Another thing to consider once you settle in to college is that while you'll keep some of your old friends, you may find that you've outgrown some of your high school connections. That's not to say you'll want to drop these friendships but that you may want to reevaluate spending as much time on them now that you've moved on to your new life. That's the case with Bella, a student new to the University of Delaware.

Since she lived in New York City most of her life, the suburban campus felt more sedate and laid back. She made new friends during orientation week and after a while started questioning whether a couple of her old friendships were right for her. It wasn't that she considered herself superior because her friends, Lacy and Maura, attended community college rather than a large university like the one she chose, or that they'd already committed themselves to lifetime relationships with their high school sweethearts.

The more Bella hung out with them when she returned home for high school homecoming, get-togethers at their houses, and shopping trips to the mall, the more she saw that they didn't have as much in common as she'd thought. She decided to spend more time on campus with some new friends she'd met by joining the future nurses' club. Like Bella, their goal was getting a rewarding job, finding an apartment, and traveling rather than getting married to their longtime boyfriends immediately after graduation.

In turn, Lacy and Maura found new friends at community college with more common interests and decided to let their high school friendship with Bella take its natural course. They'd still remain friends with

Bella but would enrich their lives by letting new people with whom they shared common goals and interests into their small circle of friends.

Bella's new way of looking at friendships paid off. She and her new friends graduated nursing school, immediately found jobs, and signed up to share an apartment. They planned vacations for the same time and decided to see the west coast before traveling with a tour group overseas. Bella still keeps in touch with her old friends, who are reevaluating their own romantic relationships and, thanks to Bella's example, are making plans to live independently before committing themselves to anyone permanently.

If you're lucky enough to already know some students you're going to college with, you're at an advantage because it will give you a sense of familiarity. That's comforting because you'll have someone with whom you can discuss concerns or problems that arise in those crucial first few weeks and throughout your college years.

If you're starting from scratch and don't know anyone from your college, expect that you'll face an adjustment. You had your own niche in high school. You may have participated in sports, joined school clubs, and enjoyed having your own circle of friends, and you may have a meaningful romantic relationship. Now, you're starting fresh. You'll still keep the friends that were important to you, but you'll find it an adventure to make new ones. Of course, all this takes time and effort on your part. Be willing to meet new friends by putting yourself out there in a friendly, caring way.

Freshman orientation presents many opportunities to make new friends. It also helps if, early on, you find out which student groups that reflect your interests would be a good fit for you. These student groups run the gamut from sports, newspaper, and drama to ones with a philanthropic leaning, like volunteer work.

If you're connected to a religion, find out about services and introduce yourself to the school chaplain. See if joining one of these organizations is right for you as they can offer you a home base and advice where you can forge friendships with like-minded students when you're away from home.

Once you feel comfortable in your surroundings and find time, stop by the commons area in your dorm. You'll meet people with similar interests and learn about events around campus. Make friends, but always use caution and good judgment to ensure that your new acquaintances are honest and trustworthy, the types of people you'd feel comfortable with as friends. It takes a while to get to know what a person's about, and you don't want to get involved with someone before you know their full story.

For example, you don't want to hang out with a party animal who would distract you from making good grades or with someone who abuses substances. Also, beware of edgy people who spill out their entire life story with all the raw parts during your first meetings. Make friends, but proceed wisely.

MAKE FRIENDS THROUGH WORK AND VOLUNTEERING

Once you've established a study schedule and find it manageable, you may find that a part-time job presents you with another chance to make friends. Think about working in a campus office, the bookstore, the dorm lobby desk, or the cafeteria. If you work in the cafeteria, you'll get free meals and more exercise than you would lounging around the dorm during your down time. You'll make extra cash and find new friends with a positive work ethic who share common goals.

Volunteer opportunities also abound in college, and it's an excellent way to make new friends. Most college students are pressed for time with full course loads and part-time jobs. Once you've set up a schedule, try finding a few hours a week to volunteer. However, you may want to wait to volunteer until you're more entrenched in your college experience as your freshman year presents many challenges with new classes and adjustments to living arrangements. Find a chance to do volunteer work sometime during your college years as it will enrich your life and help you in the coming days.

You'll find that many colleges offer credit for volunteer hours. When you choose to volunteer, think of pairing the activity with your future career, even if you have only a general field in mind for your life's work. Volunteering will help you solidify your ideas for a major and will give you more confidence in dealing with people in school and on the job.

Prospective employers will view you favorably, and you'll gain practical experience in an area that interests and excites you. You may want to consider tutoring students from a local elementary or high school, particularly if a career in teaching or counseling interests you. Students can meet you at the campus library so you don't have to travel.

You could volunteer with a food bank or soup kitchen, which would help boost a social work or human services career. Maybe you're interested in helping with political campaigns and activities, which lends itself to a career in law or politics. Pair your volunteer experience to something you're passionate about that may eventually become your life's work. You'll help yourself as well as help others. Most prospective employers prefer students who volunteer. It's a plus for your résumé.

When you first get to college, devote time to finding a network of friends you can talk to easily and run things by if you're not sure about what to do. You and your new friends can provide a home base for each other, like a family would. Of course, you'll still rely on help and advice from your family and friends back home, but you and your new friends will form a bond to take you and them through the challenges you'll face during your college years. Like high school friendships, many of your newly forged college friendships will last a lifetime.

TAKEAWAYS

- Make New Friends but Keep the Old
- Don't Make Decisions Based on Life Before College
- Join a Club to Find New Friends
- Be Prepared for a Post High School Adjustment
- Make Friends Through Work or Volunteering

DISCUSS

- Give an example of making a decision based on life before college. Why is it best not to do this?
- What types of clubs or organizations can you find at college? Which ones would interest you most and why?
- Which types of adjustments to college concern you most? Where can you find support for these issues in the college you're planning to attend?

Chapter 3

Love Your Living Arrangement

COMMUNITY COLLEGE VERSUS
A 4-YEAR COLLEGE

These days, many students start out as commuters from home or their own apartment and attend a community college for the first two years of their college career. Going to a community college for a couple of years can save you money on tuition and can help you gradually ease in to an academic and social routine you can easily manage without feeling overwhelmed. You can take your basic courses in a relaxed setting instead of big lecture halls that universities often have. Also, it may be easier to make friends in a smaller setting like a community college.

By the time you transfer to a four-year college, you'll have had the time to think about a major. You may not feel as pressured to commit to something you're not sure about and risk losing valuable college credits.

You'll find clubs that cater to your interests in a community college just as you would in a four-year college, and you may find more available time to talk to your professors and a more relaxed environment than you would in a large institution. You'll probably find your home or apartment more conducive to studying than you would find in a busy dorm. The choice is yours whether you start out your college days in a local community college or a four-year school that's near or far from your home. Before you decide, think about what type of person you are and how you'd feel most comfortable the first two years of your college career.

LIVING ON OR OFF CAMPUS

Most college freshmen live in dorms, although some choose to commute from their home to campus. By junior year, some students opt to set up their own apartments off campus, depending on college rules and their personal preferences.

Students who commute do so for different reasons. Some do it to save money. Others find that living at home gives them better conditions for quiet study time. For married students, commuting is usually their only option. If you commute by train or bus, you can use the time to catch up on assignments. As a commuter you need to be very conscious of time management since you may have additional responsibilities such as a job and family. Even though you live off campus, take advantage of forging friendships with your classmates and join study groups, which will help you keep up your grades.

Unless it's absolutely necessary, opt for a dorm room, at least for your first two years, to take advantage of having access to your professors and college resources, such as the library and study groups. If you start college by living in a dorm, you'll experience many activities you wouldn't have access to if you commuted, make new friends, and have easier access to support services, such as counseling. Sometimes all it takes is a few sessions with a counselor to help you adjust to a new way of studying and living or to find answers to your personal problems, which often magnify when you're away from home, trying to find your way in new territory.

Also, if you live on campus, your professors will be more readily available should you need their help. You can learn a lot from your professors both inside and outside the lecture hall.

Some professors meet informally with small groups of students outside of class in the lounge or coffee shop to shed more light on their subjects or to discuss current happenings on or off campus, or other issues that impact students' lives. You can learn much from these informal sessions, sometimes more than you can in class.

Some students who live on campus choose to pledge a sorority or fraternity, which presents advantages and disadvantages. Joining one can give you a built-in network of friends with whom you can socialize and study. On the other hand, if you associate with these friends to the exclusion of making friends outside your network, you may limit the experiences that would bring you a more expansive and enlightening college adventure.

Whichever way you choose to go, open yourself to many social experiences with a diverse group of students to enrich your college years. Having a wide circle of friends can also help open you up to future career choices and opportunities. Avail yourself of activities that can provide you with a satisfying social life and open doors for you regarding your future profession and graduate school.

WHAT IF YOU HAVE THE ROOMMATE FROM HELL?

You may not meet your roommate until orientation. Sometimes you'll hit it off immediately, and other times you'll find you have nothing in common, but in time, you'll learn to co-exist, mostly by going your own ways. In most cases, you and your roommate will learn to live with one another peaceably despite your individual preferences, quirks, and foibles.

You may find that you enjoy each other's company and become lifelong friends. Having a roommate is one of the most broadening experiences you'll gain from college, one that you'll carry with you for the rest of your life. You'll gain valuable life lessons such as the art of compromise and give-and-take that you wouldn't experience if you never lived with another person who was a complete stranger.

The worst-case scenario that some students encounter is being thrown together with the roommate from hell. Even if you don't believe in hell, you've heard about it in church or from your parents. You don't want to go there. Having the roommate from hell can be almost as horrific.

If your roommate keeps you awake at night with loud music, animated phone conversations, or insists on entertaining a love interest in your room while you're studying for a big exam, that qualifies as an unacceptable roommate. The most important thing you can do if your roommate makes it impossible to co-exist peaceably is to try talking to them and to compromise on a living arrangement that would satisfy both of you.

After a few days of living with her roommate, Kylie, Maria felt that she had to get out of her campus living arrangement. If ever there was a roommate from hell, Maria thought Kylie fit the description. She stayed up late talking loudly to her friends on her cell. Just last week she invited her boyfriend Jake from her hometown to visit. They spent the night making out in the bed next to Maria. Luckily, they spared her from seeing the details of their romantic tryst as they cuddled under Kylie's covers, but Maria knew they were engaging in what her grandma called "heavy petting."

After Jake left the next day, Maria told Kylie they needed to talk.

Kylie shot back. "Why are you so bent out of shape? Jake and I have been together since high school. You're a big girl now. Just close your eyes if something bothers you."

Maria sat across from her and looked her in the eye. "Kylie, things haven't been good with you and me from the beginning. I tried to put up with your loud phone calls all hours of the night, your stomping around with your Zumba videos when I'm trying to sleep, but your inviting Jake here to share our room was a deal-breaker."

Kylie gave her a look. "It's my room too."

Maria shot her a look back. "I know that, and I've tried to get along with you, but it's not working for either of us."

"Can we at least talk about it?" Kylie said in a slightly lower voice.

Maria sighed. "The only thing I can agree to is if you say you'll give me a break with the loud night talks and the exercise tapes when I'm trying to sleep. Mostly, I don't want Jake here again. That stuff belongs in a private place, like a hotel, not in a room you're sharing at college."

Kylie shook her head. "That's not going to happen, Maybe I can agree to turn down the loud talking and the salsa music, but I'm not going to tell Jake he can't visit."

"Okay, then," Maria said. "You've made your decision, and I'm making mine."

"Miss Goody-two shoes has spoken. So, what are you going to do about it?

"At orientation they told us that if we have a problem with a room-mate, we should talk to our roommate and see if we can work it out. I tried to do that, but it looks like you aren't willing to discuss it. If that didn't work, they said we should contact the resident advisor to see if they could mediate the situation for us. The next step would be to go to the director. Are you willing to see the resident advisor later today to see if she can help us? If you are, I'll set up a meeting."

"You've got to be kidding. She'll laugh in your face."

Maria grabbed her purse. "It looks like you don't want to solve this problem. I'm going to see the RA now and see if we can work something out. Do you want me to go alone, or will you go with me?"

"Okay, if you insist. But I think you're exaggerating this whole thing way out of proportion. Let me get ready, and I'll meet you at the RA's office."

In a few minutes, Maria and Kylie knocked on the RA's door, and she agreed to talk to them. They each got a chance to voice their concerns to Jade, the RA. Maria told her side of the story about how Kylie chatted loudly on her cell phone to various friends into the wee hours of the morning. She talked about Kylie's boyfriend's sleep-overs and how she felt he didn't belong in their room because it was an invasion of her privacy that was making her feel uncomfortable and embarrassed.

Kylie countered with how she wasn't happy with Maria as a roommate because she criticized her for everything and tried to take away her basic rights.

"I hear both of you," Jade said, documenting the situation in a notebook for her records. "The only way to solve this is for you, Kylie, to give Maria the peace of mind she expected when she entered this university as a dorm student."

Kylie scoffed. "What exactly does that mean?"

"Simply this," Jade said with authority, "No more loud phone conversations when she's trying to sleep and no boyfriend visits that would cause her discomfort."

"And if I don't give in to her outrageous demands?" Kylie asked.

"Then we'll take it up with our resident director, who will not look upon your actions favorably."

"I'll have to think about it and get back to you," Kylie said.

"There's nothing to think about," Jade said. "We can solve this problem today. If you agree to the terms we set, I won't report this incident to the resident director. Doing that would go on your college record, which I don't believe would help you in your grad school aspirations or future career."

After a few minutes of grousing and complaining, Kylie looked up. "Okay. Have it your way, but as soon as another dorm opens up, I'm out of there."

"That's not going to happen until next semester," Jade said, "so you'll both have to make the best of it."

Maria and Kylie had a tense but livable relationship until the next semester came (it couldn't be soon enough for both of them). Kylie got another room with a friend she knew from high school. Maria and her new roommate get along beautifully and respect one another's boundaries.

The bottom line is that most students get along with their roommates, and those who don't have ready recourse by addressing any problems with their resident advisor, resident director, or counseling center. Having a roommate can enrich your life, but it's important to set the ground rules with them at the outset. From the beginning, be sure to discuss who is responsible for certain chores, sleeping conditions, phone use, when and how often you'll entertain guests in your room, and how you'll solve disagreements.

The sooner you have a frank discussion about these and other issues important to both of you, the sooner you'll forge a compatible relationship to help you both enjoy your roommate experience to the max. That means a more relaxed and peaceful college experience for both of you in which both of you can realize your full academic and social potentials.

TAKEAWAYS

- Community College or 4-Year College?
- Living on Campus vs Commuting
- Is Joining a Sorority or Fraternity for You?
- Dealing with a Difficult Roommate
- Find Recourse if You Have a Roommate Problem

DISCUSS

- What type of college do you plan to attend? What questions do you have about this type of college? Why do you feel it's the right choice for you?

- What are your thoughts about joining a fraternity or sorority? Do you prefer having a wide circle of friends or belonging to a smaller group? Is it possible to have both types of friendships?
- What resources at college can help you if you face a problem with a roommate?

Chapter 4

Ask for Help When You Need It

CONNECT WITH YOUR ADVISOR

When you're starting a new journey like going to college, problems that seemed easy to solve while you were living at home may suddenly morph into gigantic and overwhelming problems. It's perfectly natural that challenges you face may magnify when you move into a completely new setting away from the comfort and support of your family and friends you've had for years.

But no worries, you can find the support you need whether you're moving to a sprawling urban campus or a small, tree-lined college far from the maddening crowd, even if you don't know a single person there and feel a little lost for a while. If you're a commuter, moving every day between two worlds and trying to balance work, the security of your home life, and your new college environment, the challenges facing you when a problem arises may prove even greater.

Establish a close rapport with your academic advisor from Day 1. This vital connection will take you under their wing and tell you which courses you need to take to gain your diploma every step of the way. That said, it's vital to keep signed records of all the courses they recommend taking each semester. If you decide you'd rather change any part of your course of study, be sure to consult your advisor first, and get it in writing every time. You never know when an advisor may take another job or retire, and you want to be sure all your records are in perfect order.

Be sure to document and date any conversations with your advisor about your curriculum in writing. If you're not sure of something your advisor tells you, check with the dean's office. You don't have to say anything about your advisor telling you to take certain courses. Say that you're verifying school policy.

A colleague recently said that when she attended a large university her advisor mistakenly told her that she could take two pass/fail courses. It turns out that the advisor didn't know that two pass/fail courses weren't allowed in the same semester. This student would find herself almost a credit short in her program if she hadn't verified with a reliable source what the advisor said.

Another student experienced a problem in a graduate school doctoral program with an advisor who told him to take two more graduate courses when he'd already completed all course requirements and comprehensive exams (it's well-known that students don't have to take more courses after passing comprehensives).

A friend of this student, a high school assistant principal, who was also in the doctoral program, stated that this advisor did not help many students, including her, get through the program and that she graduated with a "Certificate of Advanced Graduate Study" instead of the doctorate she'd hoped to attain to help advance her career.

To corroborate her ideas about her advisor, she showed her friend the titles of dissertations their advisor had sponsored throughout the years, and they were minimal—hardly any in the past few years. The friend she advised thought about dropping out of the program and gaining a certificate of advanced graduate study instead of the advanced degree, believing that he'd be in grad school an interminable amount of time if he continued working with this advisor. In the end, he decided to change advisors, but before making that risky decision since he'd already spent a lot of time and money on the program, he ended up taking two more courses even though his advisor had put everything in writing. Luckily, another professor agreed to accept him as an advisee, and he completed the program.

The bottom line is be sure you get everything in writing, and if you change advisors, make them aware of any dealings with your previous one. Your academic plan is the roadmap for how you'll finalize everything so that you graduate and don't get hit with any unwelcome surprises, like having to go an extra semester or taking more courses.

On the positive side, your advisor is the best person to lead you to support services that will help you with any problems that come up, both personal and school-related. In addition to consulting family and friends at home and those you've made in college, there are many professionals on campus trained to help, should you need their expertise.

Whether you're the type of person who likes to go it alone when you have a problem, or one who doesn't hesitate to ask for help when you need it, you may find a situation as a college student in which you have to ask for assistance regarding your academic or personal life. Where can you turn?

FIND SUPPORT FOR PHYSICAL AND EMOTIONAL ISSUES

Maybe you're not feeling well physically in the first few months of college. Your stomach acts up, you're experiencing anxiety, or you're getting headaches. The first place to head is your campus health center where caring professionals will help resolve your issues that may be brought on by the stress of getting used to a new environment and a way of processing information that differs substantially from what you experienced in high school.

Taking meticulous class notes and studying for tests that encompass a tremendous amount of material presents an entirely different method than what you've faced throughout your previous years of schooling. If the health center can't resolve your problem, they will refer you to more specialized medical professionals who can address the problem more specifically.

ADDRESS MENTAL HEALTH ISSUES

The counseling center at your college also offers mental health services which will benefit you if you need help managing your emotions due to issues in your personal life or those brought on by the stresses and strains related to adjustments to college life, such as living in a dorm, where privacy is hard to come by; professors whose approach to the subject differs from what you've experienced in high school; and a course load you may find difficult and unmanageable.

You can solve some of these problems by talking to your RA, your academic advisor, or your individual professors. These people are more than willing to listen to your concerns and address them. Ask for help, and explain your problem clearly and honestly. These college workers will not judge you and are there to answer your questions, but you have to ask. They won't know if something's bothering you unless you clarify what it is.

If discussing your situation with the first line of personnel doesn't help, talk to a mental health professional on campus. This is particularly important if you have a serious problem, such as substance abuse, or if you suffer from a mental health issue like anxiety or depression. If you've experienced a personal emotional upset due to a romantic break-up, a chronic illness, a death in the family, or any other problem that causes you emotional discomfort, don't hesitate to seek help to avoid worsening the emotional effects on you. You need to diminish stress in your life in order to function as a college student, a role that has its own stressors that requires a clearly focused mind and body.

Here's an example of a college student who sought help for a problem that caused him to feel anxious and depressed. Trey is an incoming freshman at a small college in a neighboring state five hours away from his home. For the past year his father has received radiation treatments, since he can't tolerate chemotherapy, for lung cancer that has progressed to Stage 4.

Trey is particularly upset because his father never smoked. Since he entered high school, Trey and his dad's relationship has deteriorated due to conflict and disharmony over Trey's desire to do things his own way and become more independent due to his dad's domineering personality. However, since his father's diagnosis, the two have done their best to make up for lost time and live in relative harmony.

Because of the history of bad blood between them before his Dad's illness, Trey suffers from guilt and remorse that interferes with his ability to concentrate on his studies and to maintain a high enough GPA to eventually apply to medical school. Trey's father will soon enter hospice care, and the college freshman can't seem to pull himself together enough to meet the demands of his work-study program, his rigorous course load, and helping his father through the final months of his illness, Trey wasn't sure where to turn for help, but he knew that if he didn't get it soon, he'd fail his first semester. He found it hard to sleep and suffered from anxiety attacks. He confided in the nurse at the health center about his emotional state after she noticed how unfocused and anxious he seemed when she gave him medication for a sore throat.

She asked if he'd be willing to speak to a psychologist at the college counseling center about his unbearable emotional state. At first, he refused, concerned that his health history would go on his permanent record. He didn't want anything to stop him from his goal of becoming a doctor. The nurse reassured him that everything would remain confidential and that he had no reason to worry. The next day, he met with Amy, a psychologist trained to deal with the stresses Trey dealt with daily.

Amy set up a series of meetings in which she and Trey discussed his ambivalent feelings about his dad over the years, his father's terminal illness, and his difficulty coming to terms with his father's impending death. The counselor advised Trey to have frank discussions with his dad about how much he appreciated the good times they spent together and how much he'd learned from his father that he'd always carry with him.

Trey also mentioned the times they didn't get along and expressed regret and remorse. He knew that it happened in the past and that he couldn't take it back. He told his dad he wanted to move ahead and think about what they could do to make the quality of their lives better for both of them. He tried to reassure his dad by saying that no one really knows how much time anyone has left on this earth, but that he planned to make the best of it and hoped his dad would too.

As it turned out, Trey's father survived longer than the doctors predicted, and they had enough time to reconcile and make good memories together. With Amy, the counselor's help, Trey was able to find a sense of equilibrium despite the fact that his father's health was deteriorating and he knew there wasn't much time left for them to be together. He found a sense of purpose in knowing that they could talk about anything now that Trey had taken the first steps to clear the air. His father spent his remaining days telling Trey how happy he was to have his son back and how he believed that Trey would reach his goal of graduating college, going to medical school, and becoming a physician.

Regardless of what your emotional issues involve, anxiety related to a family member's illness, like the one Trey experienced, or psychological symptoms related to new and challenging experiences as a college student, find the counseling center and ask for help. If you're not sure where to turn, ask your advisor or the health center staff.

Sometimes your need for support can relate to a problem in learning how to cope with your new college routine. Recognize that you're experiencing many changes all at once and that the more support you get, the better you'll be able to overcome this period of adjustment, and in your own time, flourish.

CONSULT A PEER COUNSELOR

Another helpful resource for new and established students on many campuses is the peer counseling center. You'll find fellow students from undergraduate and graduate programs, those closest to your situation and age, best equipped to discuss your issues and individual situations. They can offer you good advice from their own experiences and talk to you in a language you'll easily understand.

If your problem is more complex like Trey's, you'd be better served by seeing a professional counselor with a wide range of experience dealing with complex situations like a loved one's serious illness. Peer counseling in cases of ordinary problems of adjustment, such as not relating to a professor's teaching methods or tips for time management and studying effectively, are often easily addressed with trained peer counselors. After going through peer counseling, you may find yourself wanting to join this service to help other students.

VISIT THE CAMPUS MINISTRY

Remember Tomás in chapter 2 who found new friends by joining a club connected to the campus ministry? These faith-based organizations can help with any problems you face throughout your college years. People in charge there can counsel you or recommend additional help for academic or emotional issues should you require it. The campus ministry often provides a home away from home where you can go to feel safe and appreciated for who you are.

Even if you don't attend a religious-affiliated college, most campuses represent many different faiths, and you'll probably find yours there.

The religious leader in charge is trained in helping students with every-day adjustment issues, and sometimes, heavier ones. They can also direct you to clubs and activities that will help you find a place with like-minded people that bring you a sense of familiarity and comfort.

CHECK OUT THE TUTORING CENTER

If you're having difficulty with one or more of your subjects, visit your college's tutoring center that will help explain the subject matter you don't understand and will also offer techniques to help you pass essay and/or objective tests in subjects you find challenging. Ava sought help from the tutoring center when her English composition teacher deducted points for her literature exam. She answered the question about poetry analysis well, but when she had to write essay answers, grammar and punctuation posed problems.

Ben, a senior English major who worked at the tutoring center, told Ava that if she wasn't sure about the rules of punctuation to think about where to pause or when her voice rises or falls when she talks. In most cases she'd know where to place commas by trying this simple technique. Ben also told her to avoid dashes and exclamation points as it makes writing look unprofessional. He also advised her against writing overly long sentences and paragraphs as people like to read easily understandable text that's simple to process.

After looking over a few of Ava's essay answers, Ben said that in grammar, just because something sounds right it isn't necessarily the correct expression to use. For example, Ava had trouble using pronouns. She'd write, "Mom made a cherry pie for my friend and I" because she thought it sounded more grammatical. Ben initiated a discussion about pronoun case and discussed object pronouns and how they always appear after a preposition.

Then Ada realized that it should be "Mom made a cherry pie for my friend and *me*, not *I*." Ben said she should test each pronoun by putting a preposition before it. She then realized that the correct pronoun was *me*, not *I,* and she's been testing her pronouns ever since.

There were so many points of grammar and punctuation that Ava couldn't recall (actually, she never paid much attention to it in high school) that Ben gave her a few books that would help her review basic

English style and usage. Armed with his advice and the books, she improved her writing style. By the end of the course, she received a *B* in her English class with Ben's help and her own efforts.

You never have to go it alone whether you're a commuter or live at college. There's always help for you on campus if you have a physical or emotional problem. Talk to your advisor (a good place to start), or visit the health or counseling center if you need help right away. The campus ministry's door is always open to you, and your peers are there to make sure you succeed. Everyone on campus is rooting for you. All you have to do is ask for help, but you have to be the one to take the first step. No one will know if you have a problem if you don't take the initiative and tell them.

If you find it hard to excel in your classes, visit your professors first and ask their advice. That will let them know you want to do something about your problem with the subject matter. Then you could visit the tutoring center or find a study group. If you're having a serious issue, find a private tutor through the university. Most of the time free college resources can help you. Whatever you do, don't give up. There's always someone to help, but you have to initiate it.

TAKEAWAYS

- Connect with Your Advisor
- Get Everything from Your Advisor in Writing
- Ensure You're Getting Good Advice from Your Advisor
- Deal with College Stress Constructively
- Seek Immediate Help for Mental Health Issues
- Peer Counselors Can Offer Help for Less Serious Issues
- Use the Campus Ministry as a Resource for Problems
- Consult the Tutoring Center for Help with Courses
- Know When to Seek Help and Where to Find It

DISCUSS

- Why is it important to keep dated records and to get everything in writing when you meet with your advisor about your courses and curriculum?
- If you come up against mental health issues in college, which resources on campus can help you deal with them?
- What is peer counseling, and how can it help you?
- How can the tutoring center offer you assistance?
- What services does the campus ministry offer students?
- Where could you turn if you felt that any of these resources fell short of helping you?

Chapter 5

Practice Self-Care

BALANCE WORK AND PLAY

If you practice self-care from Day 1, you'll perceive your college experience as more satisfying, get better grades, and find your adventure a much smoother ride than if you left everything to chance. One thing you can start doing immediately is set up a system for balancing work and play.

Your college schedule will differ considerably from your high school routine. While you used to attend the same class every day at the same time and take five or six classes a day, in college you may go to class two or three days a week and take two or three classes each day. That means your workload will be heavier, and you'll have to absorb more material in a shorter amount of time.

Because your schedule will change from what you're used to, you'll want to pay more attention to maintaining a balance in your activities. You may be tempted to devote more time to schoolwork because your new routine seems more demanding due to a new way of approaching your classes, but it's also important to make time to relax and spend time doing what you enjoy. This ensures a better mental and physical outlook that will help you flourish and excel in your subjects.

With being away from home and gaining newfound freedom, it's tempting to stay up late, depriving yourself of valuable sleep, or to go out and party until the wee hours. In the end, doing things against your good judgment takes its toll on your body and mind. Keeping late hours, eating foods that aren't healthy on the run, and cramming for exams can eventually catch up with you and cut into your goals and peace of mind.

There are so many new things to experience in college that it's tempting to keep late hours just as it is to go out and not worry when you have to be home, as you did in high school. A steady diet of junk food or not sticking to regular meal times can bring you discomfort and cut down on your energy levels, which you need now more than ever to keep up with your busy schedule. If you can't get the rest you need in your dorm room, request a quiet dorm next semester.

TAKE TIME TO REST AND RECOUP

You can also make time for a short rest period during the day, a mini nap, or find a meditation you like that will calm your stress and give you a short break. You can add any kind of meditation you like to your routine. Be sure you have a quiet place so no one will disturb you; if you can't find that in your room, head to the library or a place you know you can find privacy on your campus.

You may want to choose a mantra mediation, where you repeat a word that could be a word with no particular meaning that sounds pleasant, or you can choose a word like *sun* or *happy* that has a pleasant connotation that holds meaning for you. If you're religious or spiritual, you can choose a word or phrase prayer or affirmation as your mantra. You may also try a mindfulness walking meditation where you focus on each step you take in the here and now.

Another option is to do a meditation which requires finger motions as you say words to relax you. Kirtan Kryia meditation involves touching each finger to the thumb and saying a mantra to relax you as you do the motions. These last two types of meditation are particularly helpful if you find it hard to sit without moving some part of your body, like your legs in walking or your fingers, while doing the Kirtan Kryia. You can find information about all types of meditation by looking online and watching videos to help you choose the type that's right for you.

The main thing to make you feel balanced and less stressed is to rest when you need to and not to push yourself to keep going when you're totally exhausted and your body tells you to relax because you can't run on empty. You'll accomplish more in the long run if you listen to your body and don't pressure yourself beyond your limits.

EAT HEALTHY FOODS

By now you've been warned by family and friends about the "freshman 15," or worse, "the freshmen 50." So many new college students throw caution to the wind and aren't careful of their diet, especially when eating at the buffets many meal plans include or drinking more alcohol. Many college students return home packing a few more pounds and they can't imagine how it happened.

One way to avoid extra weight gain when starting college is to be conscious of how your new food options, mainly dorm food, will broaden your waistline and turn your muscles to flab. The most important thing you can to avoid packing more pounds is look for healthy foods and think when you eat rather than wolfing down your food, no matter how hungry you are. Practice mindful eating and allow time to savor each bite rather than being unaware that you've polished off a half pound burger and a double order of fries or a large pizza with the works.

SHORT-ORDER DORM COOKING LINKS

To get a break from calorie-laden dorm food, you may want to do some short-order cooking in your room. Beside the basic dorm refrigerator and microwave, many colleges offer additional food prep items, such as a coffee maker. Some colleges also allow students to bring a hot pot to boil water for instant coffee and hot chocolate, a microwave, and a mini electric grill. If there's a microwave in your room you can buy a microwave pasta maker, a handy gadget that makes perfect pasta.

You can sauté an assortment of fresh vegetables on your grill and serve them with interesting flat breads or crackers. Check with your student handbook or your RA to see which appliances are permitted if you're not sure. Find links on the internet for interesting recipes you can make in dorm room or a commons lounge that offers cooking facilities. Here are a few to get you started:

https://food.allwomenstalk.com/avoid-the-freshman-by-learning-to-cook-these-dorm-friendly-meals/

https://www.tasteofhome.com/collection/easy-recipes-youll-actually-want-to-make-in-your-dorm-room/

https://www.allrecipes.com/article/easy-dorm-room-meals-ready-in
-minutes/

https://www.allrecipes.com/recipe/47194/devs-dorm-room-casserole/

KEEP MOVING

There's a greater temptation to become more of a couch potato when you have to read, study, and sit at your computer desk for long periods of time. It's easier to lie around in your dorm room and watch TV or listen to music when you finally find a few minutes to yourself. Exercise can become more of a chore when you have less motivation to do it because you're wiped out from trying to fit more hours into your day. Ironically, exercise can kick in and energize you more than if you remained in a prone position in your room or the lounge.

The most important factor in sticking with exercise is to find one you love and do it regularly. Pencil it into your assignment calendar if you need a strong reminder. Better yet, make plans to meet up with a friend to plan and carry out your program. Group exercise is a great option that makes you forget you're exercising because you're having fun with your friends. If you can't find a class on campus or a friend to walk with regularly, check out exercise videos that appeal to you.

You'll find a selection of YouTube videos on your computer that offer energizing Zumba routines. Many take half an hour or less. Choose longer or shorter ones that complement your schedule. It's best to exercise at least three days a week; leave a day between sessions to make it manageable and fun.

MAKE TIME FOR FUN

As discussed in chapter 2, you'll have many opportunities to meet friends through clubs and campus-sponsored events and activities. You can also make new friends in the dining hall, campus lounge, or library. You'll find new friends, who may become lifelong friends in the most unlikely places. Study groups are a great place to make friends who are willing to share their knowledge and ask you to share what you know with them. Movie nights and sporting events also offer great opportunities to meet new people.

You may be the type of person who feels comfortable having a small circle of people to hang out with, or you may enjoy splitting your time among different groups of friends. Whatever your preference, it's important to have a support system you can rely on throughout your college career. Many of the friends you make in college will remain your friends for life. Some students prefer to associate with students from different groups, while others like the comfort of joining an organization of people with common interests. It's your choice.

It's important to strike a happy balance with social life. Make time to cultivate and enjoy the benefits of an active social life, but do it with an eye on maintaining a good cumulative average and paying attention to your studies and career goals.

MANAGE YOUR TIME TO THE MAX

When you think about practicing self-care, it's important to consider how you manage your time. That means thinking about ways you can find more time in your day to study, relax, and spend time doing things you love. In order to do that successfully, think of ways you can squeeze more time into your day without sacrificing any of the things that you find important.

Think about what things you're doing that you can omit from your daily routine that eat away at your time so you feel rushed and harried to get everything done. How much time do you spend on social media and watching TV? Once you're conscious of it, you can easily cut back and gain time to do the things you want.

If you tend to procrastinate, try doing your work first and getting it over with so you have more time to spend doing the things you love, like being with friends and watching sports and movies. Make use of every free moment. If you're doing laundry, bring your work along to catch up on subjects that need your attention.

It's normal to spend extra time on studying for exams when you first start college. You have to get used to learning what each professor expects from you in class participation and tests so that you can feel more at ease in meeting their expectations and come out on top. Once you get to that point, you can adjust your study schedule so you learn to focus on their most important points in order to approach both multiple choice and essay tests to get the results you want. Once that point comes, you'll be more confident in spending an adequate but not an excessive amount of time in understanding what your professors teach you so you perform well in their courses.

If you're a commuter, using time wisely can present more of a challenge. Often, the time spent on commuting and the distance you travel can make you more tired than if you lived on campus. Factor that in when making a time management plan. Spend time each day reviewing what you learned in class rather than cramming for upcoming tests. Look over your notes for each class and highlight what the teacher emphasized. If you do this the same day, your mind will absorb the information more effectively. Catch up with friends, but don't overdo it with spending late nights out when you have to face your classes the next morning.

PAY ATTENTION TO YOUR APPEARANCE

Often how you look to yourself and others presents a clear picture of how you feel inside and what image you want to present to everyone around you; namely, yourself, your professors, and friends. Showing an outer self that reflects your competent, confident, and caring inner self confirms to you and others a reflection of how you want the world to see you.

That's not to say you have to trade in your stressed jeans for tailored slacks or carry a briefcase instead of sporting a backpack. Look what you perceive to be your best every day. This is especially important if you have a part-time job or attend classes that could impact future career possibilities.

In line with thinking about your appearance is the importance of pampering and indulging yourself periodically. Get a manicure or pedicure or set up an exchange with a friend if you're short on funds. Maintain a flattering hairstyle that's easy to care for without spending too much time. Treat yourself to an occasional massage. It can work wonders on taut muscles and everyday tensions.

Look in the mirror. If you like what you see and it's how you want the world to see you, it will help you grow in confidence and accomplishment. If you're not happy with your appearance, think of how you can show your best self to yourself and everyone around you. Your mental state will improve dramatically, and you'll show off your best attributes to lead you to success in college and in life.

TAKEAWAYS

- Balance Work and Play
- Make Time to Relax, Recoup, and Have Fun
- Eat Healthy Foods
- Take a Break from Dorm Foods
- Keep Active
- Find an Exercise You Love and Do It Regularly
- Manage Your Time Wisely
- Review Regularly Rather than Cram
- Pay Attention to Your Appearance

DISCUSS

- What are some steps you can take to help yourself relax when things become stressful in college?
- What type of physical activity do you most enjoy? What kinds of activities can you try in college to help you stay fit?
- What are some good ways to help you manage time so that you can fit in study time along with doing things you enjoy?
- Why does it help you to look your best in college?

Chapter 6

Make the Most of Class Time

KEEP YOUR EYES AND EARS
ON THE PROFESSOR

Many students don't grasp how important it is to give strong attention to what their professors say during lectures, in addition to watching their body language and reading between the lines when they teach and during interactions with the class. Some college students are new to note-taking and write down everything the teacher says instead of concentrating on recording what the teacher considers most important. Also, a lot of students focus mainly on textbook materials at the expense of truly hearing what their teachers emphasize. It's equally important to give attention to handouts as this material that professors consider important often shows up on tests.

How do you know what your teachers want you to remember from their lectures to help you do well in their tests? For one thing, watch body language, like direct eye contact (indicates something's important) and steepling (making a steeple with fingers, indicating your prof is an authority on this topic and expects you to be too). Listen for changes in tone of voice, including pauses and emphatic speech, which tells you the teacher wants to emphasize something.

If they say, "Remember this," "I repeat," "This is important," or a similar phrase, remember what they say. It will likely show up on your exam. When they stress certain points you think they want you to remember from their lectures, be sure to refer to it in your essay test answers or remember these points for objective (true/false or multiple-choice) tests. To help you remember, place an asterisk next to that reference in your notes or highlight it. Do it as you're listening to the lecture, so you won't forget to do it later.

Similarly, if the teacher spends more time discussing or explaining one aspect of the material, copy that. On the other hand, if you waste time writing down everything they say, you'll miss the important points that may show up on a test. If you take good notes by filtering out the fluff and focusing on the important points, you'll have played the game well.

Be sure to question your teachers if they make a point and you have little or no clue about what they're talking about. Ask specific rather than general questions. Instead of saying, "What do you mean? I'm not sure I understand," say, "Can you explain more about theme in literature?" Continue asking questions until you understand. Here's a specific type of question you may want to ask to clarify the previous one. "Is the theme of a story the surface meaning or the deeper meaning, and how do I look for it?"

Ask right away if you don't understand something. Some students hesitate asking questions because they're worried about what the teacher may think about them or that the other students will not like it, but, in fact, the teacher and the other students will respect them more for asking.

TAKE GOOD NOTES

Be sure the notes you take are legible and meaningful so that when you review or study for your exams you'll have something substantial to guide you because class notes, along with handouts and your textbooks, will provide crucial information for your mastery of the subject. To take notes, use words or phrases introduced by bullets, asterisks, or dashes. That will help you whittle the information down to the bare bones. Writing complete sentence takes valuable time that you may not have, especially if your teacher talks fast.

You can eliminate the bullets or asterisks and indent each main point to save time. Also, use abbreviations that make you feel comfortable, your own personal abbreviations, so that you don't miss out when the teacher says something important. Here's what something like that might look like:

Class Notes for a Poetry Course

Imagine that your professor wants to stress certain things when analyzing poems. Use abbreviations and shortcuts you're comfortable with, like the ones you use when you take notes in class. Don't bother to put periods after your abbreviations as it takes more time away from getting everything down, and every second counts. Choose abbreviations you like, but be sure you can translate them later, and be sure you can read your writing or printing. If you're not sure about what the teacher wants you to know, ask.

Sample Notes from a Poetry Course

Introduction to Poetry Analysis

- What does title mean?
- Literal and symbolic mngs of poem
- Who is spkr and why is it mngful?
- What is theme or deeper mng of poem?

Be sure to review the professor's notes well before a test so they're imprinted on your brain. Do this as often as you can, particularly if you find the subject difficult. When exam time arrives, you'll remember those points with ease and repeat them with your own insights to impress your teachers.

KNOW WHAT TO STUDY FOR YOUR EXAM

If your teacher hasn't addressed the topic, be sure to ask which parts of the textbook they'll stress on your exams. Don't leave it to someone else in the class to ask, as it's important that you know how to extract what's significant enough to recall from a large body of material. Listen to verbal cues professors give about the material like, "Be sure to pay attention to (this chapter or this section)" or, "You'll want to refer to my notes and the handouts on this topic."

Since you buy your books, highlight what you think are the most important sections that you think you'll find on an exam. Use yellow markers because it's easier to read the text, and underlining can look messy when you're trying to review the material. Don't worry about reselling your textbook if you mark it up because the next person to get it will probably appreciate your highlighting the material when they study for a test.

In addition to your textbook, most teachers provide handouts, which can be valuable study aids. If you receive a lot of handouts, ask the teacher what you should stress in the handouts when you study for exams. The more clues you can get about what to study, the better. If you receive a small number of handouts, assume that all the material is important, and add it to the information you'll want to retrieve from class notes and your textbooks.

HELP! MY PROFESSOR JUST LANDED FROM THE MOTHER SHIP

Most of your professors will act and teach like other humans you know. But beware—once in a while you may find yourself with a professor from an alien nation. You'll know right away, usually from the way the prof rambles and doesn't make sense to anyone in the class. Sometimes, their demeanor and dress give them away. Dr. James Fenimore Dukon, a professor in a History of the English Language course in an urban university, sported silver hair like Albert Einstein, but a much wilder mane, like an electric shock had zapped him. That's where the resemblance ended.

This professor always wore the same rumpled tweed suit that smelled like cigars and looked like moths had nested in it. He struck his students as one of those teachers you needed to drop from your roster as soon as you could race to your advisor's office. Dr. Dukon spoke in a rambling monotone and didn't make sense to any of his bewildered sophomores as he rhapsodized in Old Norse and recited Chaucer's "Canterbury Tales" in Middle English. After one day in his presence, many students banged on their advisors' doors, begging for a transfer out of Dukon's class. Of course, in most cases the answer was *no*, so they had no choice but to stick it out.

They'd heard from other students who'd barely passed his class with a *D* that they should avoid him at all costs. Unfortunately, he was the only teacher for History of the English Language, which was a graduation requirement for all English majors. It was a lot like the swimming course in the required physical education class that everyone had to take without exception unless they had a serious physical disability. If you couldn't swim across the pool, you couldn't graduate, no matter how smart you were or how high an average you maintained.

Serena, one of Dr. Dukon's students, was lucky enough to get a dispensation from the swimming requirement because she contracted a mono virus in her freshman year. However, she ended up in a "Safety in Your Gym Class" with physical education majors instead of "Swimming Fundamentals." The professor who taught the course told Serena that she'd be the person to carry all the other students' gear that included goggles, snorkeling gear, and damp towels with which the students had wiped all the nooks and crannies of their sweaty bodies.

One day when Serena thought she'd reached her limit for tolerating the course, the teacher, who harbored a personal dislike for academic majors, told her to jump over a high wooden horse to demonstrate how to do it safely. There was no way she was going to leap over that horse, so she attempted a sexy limbo strut and meandered underneath it.

The professor stared at Serena and said, "If you ever do anything that stupid again, I'll flunk you, Ms. English major." Her classmates laughed and cheered her on until the teacher blasted them out. She ended up with a *pass* in that course. Luckily, it was a pass/fail course and didn't count toward her cumulative average. Serena believed that she'd never experience anything like that again, but now she had to deal with Dr. Dukon.

Some say that everything that happens in life has a reason. Experiencing that safety course may have prepared Serena for Dr. Dukon's course. Some students in other programs who mistakenly chose it as an English elective rejoiced when their advisors gave them a welcomed transfer slip to Victorian poetry or Advanced English Grammar. Anything was better than daffy Dukon. Advisors told students in the English education program that they had to stay with Dukon; their graduation required it if they wanted to be certified to teach.

Each day made the students in Dukon's class detest his class more. Students had a certain number of cuts for each class, and Serena said that all of them took advantage of that to meet and commiserate about him in the student lounge. Many of them forged friendships that lasted way beyond college as they were united in buoying one another up in their misery, and when the nightmare ended, sharing laughs about their experiences.

Class members couldn't begin to study for his strange multiple-choice tests that always had as options "all of the above" and "none of the above." Chaucer wouldn't be able to pass those exams. His essay tests were even worse. Here's an example Serena recalled: "Trace language development from the beginning of old English" to present-day English as we know it, and "What were the most memorable parts of my lectures about Old Norse?"

Serena said that students openly cheated on tests, but Dukon didn't seem to care. He perched in his swivel chair with his dwarf-like feet propped up on the desk and buried himself in his tattered MAD Magazine collection until it was time to turn in our tests and he shouted, "Time's up." Once the student behind Serena poked her in the back, "Psst, show me your paper. I can't get any of the blankety-blank answers."

Serena replied in a stage whisper, "Make up your own blankety-blank (fill in your favorite curse words) answers. That's what I'm doing. Don't worry about what you write. He's not going to read them anyway." The kid poked her again, harder this time, and began writing furiously.

Serena said that everyone ended up with *C's* and *D's* in Dukon's course. She felt they were lucky to survive his wild class, and most of them were happy to pass the course. When Serena asked her advisor why the university let him continue teaching, she said they didn't fire her illustrious professor because he had tenure, and despite his eccentricities, he'd know how to file a profitable law suit. Besides, his cousin held a high position in administration. Politics plays a big role in higher education, especially in graduate school, as in the example in chapter 4, about an advisor who delayed or put a stop to students attaining their doctorates.

That's why if you're a student, it's best to keep a low profile, especially when you have a complaint about a professor. Bide your time and don't make waves, unless the situation's impossible. In that case, ask the counseling center or a professor you trust for advice as they know the ins and outs of college politics. Sometimes you have no choice but to try to transfer out of the class.

GET ALONG WITH YOUR PROFESSOR
WITHOUT BEING A KISS-UP

Thankfully, most of the professors you'll meet in college, unlike Dr. Dukon, are intelligent, experienced experts in their field who relate well to students and go out of their way to help them succeed. It's important to ask about grading policies at the beginning of the course so you'll know how to proceed if you want to get a good grade.

Ask questions if you're not clear about how each component of the class counts toward your grade. You'll want to know how much class participation figures in the mix, and if it counts at all. You'll need to know about the weight of quizzes versus major tests. Also, in essay tests, how much do grammar and writing style count compared to subject matter knowledge? Find out about the teacher's office hours, should you have a question or need help throughout the semester.

Student/teacher relationships in college are much like you remember them in high school, but also different as some of your classes may be held in large, impersonal lecture halls. You'll want to maintain a good relationship with your teachers without seeming like what your parents called a brown noser.

In some of your classes, you'll find students who raise their hands constantly to flaunt their knowledge or to ask irrelevant questions. Often to the annoyance of the other students, they monopolize valuable class time to make themselves the center of attention. Most teachers know how to handle them by ignoring them or saying something like, "I need to get on with the lesson," or, "I have to give others a chance to talk." In classes where the teacher allows one or two students dominate the class, there's not much you can do, other than get the professor to answer your own questions or try to get them on another topic.

If you have more questions than you think would be fair to ask during class, visit your teacher during office hours rather than showing up uninvited. Take advantage of office hours to ask your teachers about points in their lecture or the textbook that you don't understand or may feel reluctant to ask when other students are around. If you still need help, ask the teacher for additional reading materials to supplement their lectures or textbook information and visit the campus tutoring center or the peer tutoring center. Never hesitate to ask if you don't understand something. It's important to go into tests fully confident. Once exam day arrives, it will be too late.

TREASURE TEACHERS WHO INSPIRE YOU

When you find a professor who makes the subject come alive for you or who inspires you to consider choosing a major connected to their subject, do all you can to nourish that relationship. Talk to the teacher during office hours or in informal chats about career possibilities in their field. The day may come when you'll want to ask this teacher for a recommendation to graduate school or for a job opening. Many students didn't start out wanting to be what they originally chose for a profession, but their best high school and college teachers inspired them to go that route.

Ask teachers who inspire you about job opportunities in their fields. Ask about practical issues, like job requirements, pay, and different job opportunities. Also ask about the rewards and pitfalls of choosing a career in this field. Find out how to prepare yourself for a job in this area. Determine if it's best to go to grad school after you get your bachelor's, to seek an internship, or to apply for a job and start grad school while you're working in the field.

Many people who major in education plan to begin teaching soon after graduation because some school districts would rather pay people who have fewer credentials at the outset than those who start out with advanced degrees and would command a higher salary. Think about your own future career and the best way to approach it.

Ask professors you admire and with whom you share a good rapport for their advice, even if your interest doesn't fall within their area of study. You can depend on these teachers who inspire you to give you their best advice. It's never too early to begin thinking about your future career. What better person to advise you than a professor who inspires you.

TAKEAWAYS

• Pay Close Attention during Lectures

- Watch for Verbal and Visual Clues from Your Teachers while Taking Notes
- Ask Specific Rather than General Questions about Things You Don't Understand
- Take Good Notes
- Develop your Own Shorthand System for Note-Taking
- Get a Good Idea of What to Study for your Exam
- Tolerate or Drop a Problem Professor?: It's Your Call
- Get Along with Your Professor without "Kissing Up"
- Treasure Teachers who Inspire You

DISCUSS

- How will paying close attention during lectures help you get better grades?
- What are some helpful shortcuts you can use to take good notes?
- How will you know what you need to know to study for exams?
- What can you do if you have a professor who makes your life miserable?
- How can inspiring teachers help you in your future career?

Chapter 7

Let Your Learning Style Help Boost Your GPA

WHAT ARE LEARNING STYLES, AND HOW CAN KNOWING ABOUT THEM HELP YOU?

If there's one thing all college students have in common it's their desire to get a good GPA or grade point average. It's important to know what to study, which chapter 6 addressed when talking about taking good notes in class. Add reviewing handouts and knowing what to study in the textbook to the mix, and you'll have a precise knowledge of what to study so you know you're on the right track.

Even though the knowledge you gain from your courses is just, if not more important, than getting good grades, your GPA will be a strong influence in getting you into grad school, finding the internship you're looking for, and, most important, getting your dream job.

Another way to boost your success in getting good grades is to think about and identify what type of learner you are so you know how best to go about studying most effectively to get the grades you want. The best teachers appeal to their students' different ways of learning in hopes of helping them succeed in the best way possible to reach their goals. It may take extra effort on their part, but teachers at all grade levels who take the time to identify and implement the way their students learn best have great success rates in having the most students excel in their subjects.

That said, it will help you greatly as a college student to define your main way or ways of learning that guarantee your success in achieving the grades you want. Some people have one way of learning best, while others possess a combination of two or more. After you read about the different ways people learn, you'll be able to identify your learning style and tailor how you study to how you learn best. Study time becomes less boring and more rewarding, and you reap the rewards of good grades, a victory for you.

What are learning styles and why do they matter? Back in the 1970s, the idea of recommending different learning styles to help students absorb what they learn became popular. The many proponents of learning styles chose to look at them in different ways, but they all shared some of the same basic principles. Boiled down to its bare bones, the three ways we learn are by seeing things (visual), hearing things (auditory), or touching/feeling things (kinesthetic). Although some critics blasted the idea of learning styles as unscientific, the idea remains popular today because it works.

Many teachers use the principles of learning styles and report definite progress in students who clearly identified and used their own major learning style or styles. It gives students another tool to enhance their understanding and retention of information. Therefore, it's helpful to know something about different learning modalities in your quest to understand all your college subjects and do well in them.

HOW YOU CAN MAKE YOUR LEARNING STYLE WORK FOR YOU

Are You a Visual Learner?

Figure out the way that you learn best by reading these descriptions and figuring out which types of activities best support your main learning style. You may have a combination of learning styles, but usually one predominates.

Visual learners learn best and more quickly by reading and seeing information rather than hearing it or doing hands-on activities. You're a visual learner if you learn best and more efficiently by reading, seeing, visualizing, and watching. Highlighting and underlining information helps you process it better. You can also create study cards with shortcuts to help you recall information. Index cards are good to use because they're portable since you can use them on public transportation or any time you have a free moment to devote to study. You can move the cards around to give the information that needs more study a prominent place in the order you need to study them.

Another thing you may be able to do is form pictures in your mind of the material you need to learn; in other words, visualize it. Using mnemonics (memory devices created by making up a sentence, song, or rhyme) confuses some students, but if you're comfortable with it, it can be helpful to you as a visual learner. When you watch films or videos or use charts and graphs, it also helps clarify material you want to learn. If you understand things better when you see them, you're a visual learner.

What If You're an Auditory Learner?

Auditory learners mainly lean on hearing to help them learn. Record your notes to help you remember important information. Listen carefully when your professors lecture, and ask them to explain anything you don't understand so you'll remember it better. Repeat things orally when you study.

Discuss and review work with a study group. The more you hear material repeated, the stronger your memory will be when it's time to recall it for a test. Reread your notes, handouts, and important segments of your textbook aloud. When you read the material, use great expression and emphasize the words you believe to be most important. Mnemonics, in addition to being a visual cue, can also serve people that learn toward an auditory learning style. So, start making up little sayings or poems to help you remember concepts you'd otherwise easily forget. If you understand things better when you hear them, you're an auditory learner.

What If You're a Kinesthetic Learner?

Are you a hands-on type of person, someone who likes to move around by dancing, exercising, and literally enjoys "taking a hike"? Learning by touch (kinesthetic learning) or getting into your subject with hands-on techniques is for you. One thing you can do if you're a kinesthetic learner is sit down with your notes, handouts, and textbook and write or use your computer to recopy the most important highlights of exactly what you'll need to study for your essay or multiple-choice test.

Try writing everything out by hand because some people find that extra bit of effort worth it when learning important information. However, do what works best for you. Always let that be your guide when committing something to memory or understanding concepts so you can readily relate them back in a testing situation. After you've written the most important facts and figures you want to recall, read them aloud to add an extra memory boost, no matter what kind of learner you are.

If you like to make lists, jot down a list of things to remember after each main concept. Just as when you take class notes, use a dash, asterisk, or a bullet to separate issues. Whatever you do, cut your information down to the bare bones, the most important principles, so you don't clutter your brain with extra information you don't need for the test.

It also helps to move around while you study if you're a kinesthetic learner. Avoid flopping down in your desk chair, or worse, your bed, as you may fall asleep and not wake up until the day of the test. Stretch a lot and give yourself frequent breaks (every fifteen minutes of so) to refresh your brain while you're studying. If you learn best without noise, turn off all distractions, especially your phone. Make your study sessions short so you don't get tired or bored.

While some students learn best with less noise and fewer distractions, others feel comfortable playing music or hearing noise in the background. It helps them concentrate better. You know how you learn best. Follow the method that's worked for you in the past. You're often asked when a college accepts you if you'd like to stay in a quiet dorm, where it's less hectic than the hustle and bustle of a regular dorm.

At the time, you may not think much of it, but it's an important decision you need to make for many reasons—the main one deals with what you personally need to have a positive study environment. If a noisy dorm will significantly impact your ability to concentrate, opt for the quiet dorm. If having people around you talking loudly and playing music complements your ability to study and boosts your mood, choose the regular dorm.

If you understand things better when you use a hands-on approach, you're a kinesthetic learner. You like to actually feel what's happening during the learning process and enjoy moving around rather than sitting quietly when you study. Moving, touching, and doing things gives you a sense that you're taking the material in and sinking your teeth in it, so that when you face the test, you're ready to spew out the answers with less effort.

What If It's Hard to Recall Your Material?

Have you ever come up against a situation that no matter what methods you use or how hard you study, you have trouble conjuring up the answers in a test? This happened to Darnell in a statistics class in grad school. It was hard to recall the formulas and what each of them meant because he had no frame of reference in which to put them. Statistics had nothing to do with anything in his life (he was a sociology major), but he needed to get a decent grade in the course to get through his program. Nothing seemed to work. No matter how hard he studied the formulas, he couldn't remember them.

Out of the blue it came to Darnell that other times when he was at a loss for how to recall material he needed to learn for an important test and nothing seemed to help, he resorted to memorization. That's right, good old-fashioned memorization, rote learning, like we used back in the day in grade school to memorize times tables.

When the thought of the stat midterm coming up threw Darnell into a state of acute anxiety, he decided to memorize the formulas that gave him trouble. He wrote a short explanation next to each formula based on the professor's notes. Then he made up a mnemonic device to relate each juicy tidbit of information next to each formula, so he could use it during the exam.

It worked, and Darnell passed the exam with flying colors. Even the statistics professor expressed surprise because after he helped all he could, Darnell still drew a blank when it came to recalling the basic principles he needed to know. To this day, if you ask Darnell about statistics, he still has trouble understanding it, but he also still recalls those formulas and the little sayings that he made up to exemplify them in the test.

There's always something you can do to prepare for and do well in a test. Talk to your teachers and tell them what's giving you trouble about the subject; visit the tutoring center; or join a study group. Even when everything else lets you down, there's always something new you can try to get the things you need to know into your brain so that you can make a good showing in an exam.

All you have to do is be creative and think of a method that works uniquely for you. Don't give up if you're baffled by a subject. There's always an answer. You got this far, and you'll make it through all your courses with the grades you want and deserve.

PACE YOURSELF

It's important to consider pacing when studying for exams. Some subjects will come easy to you because you enjoy studying them; others will be harder because you're not interested in them or because they present a serious challenge. Cole, a gifted high school student, texted Ms. Stein, his trusted high school English teacher, for advice when he was a college freshman. Here's their conversation about studying for college versus high school:

Cole: Studying for college is much different from studying in high school, just as you told us. I didn't know it would be so hard, trying to fit in all my subjects and play basketball. As you know, I'm on a basketball athletic scholarship, and I have to do well. To tell you the truth, I'm overwhelmed right now. It seems like no matter how much time I spend studying, I can't find time to give all my courses the attention they need.

Ms. Stein: I hear you, Cole. I know how you made straight *A*'s in high school, but as you see, it's (excuse my bad joke) a different ballgame now.

Cole: You're right. As soon as I seem to find time to study for one test, another comes up, and I can't seem to juggle my time so I can fit everything in, especially with the commitment I made to keep up my grades in exchange for the basketball scholarship.

Ms. Stein: How are you dividing your study time? How much time are you allowing to study for each subject, particularly English, because I know it wasn't your favorite subject?

Cole: I did well in your class because you spent time helping me whenever I had a problem with it. I actually began to like it. But it seems that no matter how hard I study for my courses, I fall behind. My advisor recommended the tutoring center. They're helping me with the subject, but I think that time management is more of a problem for me.

Ms. Stein: One suggestion I can offer is to spend more time on the subjects you don't relate to as much, like English and history. Math and science come easy to you, so you'll probably be okay with devoting a little less time to those subjects and spending some of the time you have left on the other two subjects. The confidence you have regarding the subjects you prefer and that you naturally do well in will carry you a long way. Of course, you need to study for them, but you already have a big body of knowledge to fall back on and a natural curiosity about math and science that makes these subjects easier for you to learn.

Cole: You're saying push back a little on the subjects I do well in and devote more time to those like English and history that I feel less confident in because they don't appeal to me as much.

Ms. Stein: Try it and see what happens. I find that many students devote a similar amount of time to preparing for all their courses when they could easily devote less to their best subjects and more to the ones that they don't care for as much.

Cole: Okay. I'll let you know how it goes. It makes sense.

Cole called Ms. Stein the following semester to say how well the plan worked for him. He budgeted his study time so that he'd devote more time to his English and history courses and less to his math and science classes. He ended up with an outstanding cumulative average his first semester that included a *B* in his composition class and an *A-* in history. As expected, Cole got two *A*'s in his math and science classes. He also had enough time to play and excel in basketball so he could move toward his dream of playing pro basketball after graduation.

Often, you'll find, as in Cole's case, that there are simple solutions to seemingly complex problems you face in college. In this situation, all it took was finding a way to manage all his subjects without sacrificing his success in any of them. Most of the time, you can find answers to any problems you face by using your common sense and confidence to arrive at an answer that's right for you. There's always an answer. If you can't find it, there are plenty of people around who can help you.

TAKEAWAYS

- Identify Your Learning Style(s): Visual, Auditory, or Kinesthetic
- Process Information by Reading, Seeing, Visualizing, Watching, or Moving

- Depend on Seeing if You're Visual
- Lean Mainly on Hearing to Help You Learn if You're Auditory
- Rely on Hands-on Experiences and Movement if You're Kinesthetic
- Having Trouble Recalling Material for a Test?: Try This.
- Pace Yourself While Studying

DISCUSS

- Explain the main learning styles. What do you consider your main learning style or styles?
- How can using activities connected to your learning style help you get good grades?
- What technique can you use as a last resort if you're having trouble remembering information for a test?
- How can pacing yourself help you do well in your exams? Give an example of pacing yourself when studying for a test.

Chapter 8

Ramp Up Test-Taking Skills

ACE TRUE/FALSE AND
MULTIPLE-CHOICE TESTS

Once you pin down the best way for you to learn (visual, auditory, or kinesthetic) and know how to pace your study time for each subject based on your interest and ability in each subject, think about how to approach the different types of tests you'll deal with during your college career. First, be sure you know what will be included in the test and what type of test it will be. Before you take the test, review test-taking skills for the type of test you're facing. Be sure not to cram before the test and get a good night's sleep the day before. Above all, don't panic, so your brain will be fresh and alert for any surprise questions.

Mainly, you'll want to know something about multiple-choice, true/false, and essay tests, three types of tests you'll most likely encounter in your courses. Although you've taken tests of like these in high school, the ones in college may cover more material and seem more challenging to you. Once you gain test-taking skills in these types of tests, you'll find taking both of them something you can easily manage.

Out of the three types of tests, true/false is probably the easiest to figure out since the answer is either right or wrong. For true answers each part of the sentence must be true. One little detail can make it false. A statement with a qualifying word, such as *sometimes*, *many*, *most*, *may*, and *often* is often true. Here's an example: Sometimes students have difficulty learning certain school subjects because the instruction doesn't match their learning style. In this case, the word *sometimes* limits the meaning of the statement and allows for exceptions, so it is true.

On the other hand, a statement that uses absolute words is usually false. These are words like *everyone, always, never,* and *only*. These words imply that there aren't any exceptions to what is stated in the question. These words can make a statement false, but not all the time. Here's an example: *Everyone* should attend college to ensure having a good career. This statement is false because not everyone needs to attend college to have a good career. In this sentence, the word *everyone* is an absolute word that impacts the meaning of the sentence to make it false. Use your judgment when figuring out whether a statement is true or false. That's the best way to decide on your answer.

For many college students, multiple-choice tests prove difficult, especially the ones that carry options for "all of the above" and "none of the above" in the same question. Concentrate on answering the multiple-choice questions you know, and leave the other ones until after you answer the ones you're sure you know. Check off the questions you're not sure about so you can easily revisit them after you answer the questions you know.

Don't spend too much time on one question. Figure out how many questions there are and how much time you have to take the test. Then estimate how much time you can realistically devote to each question. Answer the ones you're sure of first. Be sure to read the answer choices carefully and see which ones click best with the question. Try to answer the question in your mind before reading all the choices. You'll find it easier to choose the right answer that way.

For multiple-choice questions, don't leave any answers blank unless you're penalized for guessing. In most cases, you won't be. If you see an *all* or *none of the above* question, consider that if there's more than one answer you think is correct, the answer may very well be *all of the above*. Similarly, if more than one answer appears to be incorrect, consider *none of the above* a good choice.

If you're not sure of a multiple-choice answer, give it your best guess. Let your gut feeling (intuition) guide you. Also, use process of elimination when answering multiple-choice questions. If any of the answers don't seem likely to you, rule them out right away. Check off the responses that don't seem to fit. Be sure all the answers you choose pertain to the course you're taking and the information stressed by your teacher. Some of them may be trick questions that are there to distract you.

The keys to doing well in true/false and multiple-choice tests are to budget your time before you start, allowing more time for harder questions; read each question carefully; and read between the lines so you can pinpoint the right answer. Also look for clues, like qualifiers, in true/false tests, and specific wording in multiple-choice tests to help you respond correctly. Place a minus sign next to improbable choices on your test paper as you find them, so that you can narrow down the playing field to find the best answer. Use a minus sign to differentiate it from questions you need to return to later.

ANSWER ESSAY QUESTIONS WITH CONFIDENCE

Many students experience anxiety when they think about taking essay tests. If you've chosen the right material to review from lecture notes, textbooks, and hand-outs, you'll approach your essay exams with confidence. Be sure to review at frequent intervals rather than study all the material in a short amount of time. However, as with objective tests, you need to budget your time efficiently.

Since you have a time limit, it's important to budget your time before you start writing. Write your essay answers in the order that seems like the most manageable to you. When you look at your exam questions, read over each one to see which ones you can answer with the least effort. Divide your time accordingly. Some students like to answer the questions they find less difficult first, while others prefer to answer the ones they find the most difficult first. Many students say they feel more comfortable working on the ones with which they feel more confident first.

Decide how much time you want to devote to each question, based on their order of difficulty for you, and then choose your tactic. Don't spend more time than you think is reasonable for each question. First, read the question carefully, and underline the key points in the question that you need to address.

In your blue book cover or on scrap paper (ask for scrap paper if you don't get it), write an effective topic sentence for your question. Restate the question and add information about the topic that you'll include in your answer. The most important thing you need to do is answer the question directly. Do not go off on tangents or digress. Stick to answering the question, and you'll be one step ahead.

These two words contain the key to acing essay tests: *Outline first.* Many students use this technique and report that it helps them attain success in scoring well in essay exams: Here's the plan. Never start writing your answer first, not knowing where you'll end up. Always outline your essay answers on the inside covers of your blue book, if your college uses one, or use scrap paper.

WRITE YOUR ESSAY THE EASY WAY

Use the Shortcut System

A word of advice: When you take your essay test, don't freak out when you see the students around you frantically start scribbling their answers while you're still only in the planning stages of concocting yours. In the end, your planning will pay off, while more than a few of their essays will turn out discombobulated and disjointed. Follow this system, and you'll write incredible answers with this simple, yet winning, technique.

On the inside of your blue book cover or on your scrap paper, write a brief word or phrase outline (not a sentence outline as it takes too long) about all the points you'll cover in your essay answer. Don't worry about the order of the outline you'll put your ideas in until you're done listing what you think are the most important points you need to include in your essay. Write each brief idea in a row as you think of each of them. Don't number your points until you get them all down in a row.

Say you have three essay questions and have three quarters of an hour for the test. That allows you about fifteen minutes to answer each question, give or take a few minutes based on how much time you've allotted to each question after you've read all of them. Be sure to allow what you think is the best amount of time to answer each question based on your knowledge of the subject matter and your confidence in dealing with it.

Once you've written the brief outline on your blue book cover or scrap paper, number each point in your outline in a logical order. All you have to do is put numbers next to the ideas you've already written. Write succinctly and briefly, fleshing out your brief word or phrase outline. Including too many ideas in your outline may not allow you to give enough attention to the ones you've included. Write three or four points for each essay in your outline. Your outline will be your roadmap to writing a good answer for each essay.

Now it's time to write your topic sentence before you expand on it with the points in your outline. The topic sentence should contain part of the exam question and also hint at how you're going to elaborate upon it in your answer.

Tie your ideas together with transition words, such as *also, on the other hand, finally,* and *in conclusion* so that your essay answer ends up in a neat package when your teacher reads it instead of looking like disjointed sentences that don't relate to one another.

Cap off your essay in your ending sentence by referring to your topic sentence in a different, more creative way. Add an interesting fact or figure or bit of information to your concluding sentence, and presto, you've aced your essay.

Leave Time to Proofread

Many students omit this major step in the essay-writing process because they don't leave enough time, or they don't consider its importance in helping them get a good grade. It's vital that you leave time to proofread your answers for grammatical and spelling errors. Correct these errors before handing in your essays as it could mean the difference between an average grade and the one you want. Here's an easy way to do this: Start by reading to check that everything makes good sense. Check for any words you may have left out, and see if you need to use a better word in place of one you've already used.

Give your essay a quick spell check. If you don't know how to spell a word or you're not sure, use a synonym you know how to spell. Also, give your answers a quick once-over for major grammatical errors involving punctuation, like sentence fragments or run-on sentences. Remember that every sentence must have a complete thought. A fragment is part of a sentence that doesn't have both a subject and predicate (verb). A run-on sentence rambles on without proper punctuation. Also, make your essay sound professional by avoiding the second person *you* as it's too informal for an essay.

Finally, check for any glaring grammatical errors, like improper pronoun use. Here's one, mentioned in chapter 4, that many students make when they use nominative case after a preposition and say "for you and I." A lot of students fall into the trap of using a subject pronoun, *I,* because they think it sounds better than for you and *me.*

It's helpful to leave about five minutes to enhance your essay by proofreading it. If you spend less time than that, despite all your other efforts to use this shortcut system to write a stellar essay, you may not impress your professor enough to give you a good grade.

Use Shortcuts and Abbreviations in Writing Your Outline

In summary, when you write your essay answers, use your own unique shortcuts and abbreviations to write your outline. Take the time to number your points in a logical order after you've finished writing them in a word or phrase format. After you've written your essay based on your outline, add transitions, words like *also*, *on the other hand*, and *finally.* Take the time to proofread your essay, so it's as perfect as you can make it. Now it's time to hand it in and wait for your good grade to come in.

Here's a sample outline for an essay that Grace, a college sophomore, wrote in college about the significance of the green light in *The Great Gatsby.* The professor gave students a choice of three essay questions, and Grace chose this one because she enjoyed reading this novel, and it resonated with her. If you get a choice of essay questions, choose the one you can answer with confidence and ease. Grace's teacher said that students could bring the books they studied to the exam in case they wanted to check page or chapter references.

Here's the essay outline Grace uses. You can use the same easy system to outline your own essay answers. Of course, you'll use your own format and abbreviations. Here's the topic sentence Grace wrote for the essay "The Significance of the Green Light in *The Great Gatsby*":

"Although the reader is confronted with the green light on Daisy's dock only three times, the light acts as the basic symbolic and structural device, giving the novel unity and meaning." (Grace restated the question and added a hint of what she'd address in the essay.)

First, Grace wrote out all the ideas that she wanted to include in the essay. What you see is her brief outline after she rearranged the numbers to reflect the order she'd use in her essay. You can see the longer version of the outline next to the abbreviated one so you can get an idea of how to write the short version when you're pressed for time.

You'll see only the first sentence of each point in the outline. Once Grace started writing, she filled in the details for each of the points. Remember that you don't have to number your ideas until you decide the order in which you'll use them in your answer.

Outline for the Gatsby Essay Answer to write on Your Blue Book or Scrap Paper

1. G. gazes out at the grn. lt. at end of Ch.1 (Gatsby gazes out at the green light at the end of Chapter 1.)
2. In Ch. 5, grn. lt. fades. Reinforces Gatsby's feelings re D. He built an illusn. around D. (In Chapter 4, the green light fades. This reinforces Gatsby's feelings about Daisy. He built an illusion around her.)
3. Final tme. seeing green lt. at end of bk. Final image shows G's search for hope. Cite church im. of grn. for hope. (We see the green light for the final time at the end of the novel. This final image reinforces the idea of Gatsby's search for hope. We're reminded of the ecclesiastical imagery of green for hope.)

As you can see, Grace put in an extra thought in #2 and #3 in her outline so she'd remember to include it when she started writing more details in the essay. Remember that these are Grace's standard abbreviations, ones she always uses. Yours may look a lot different.

Here are the concluding two sentences that Grace wrote for her essay: "We are lifted up at the end with Gatsby as his friend assures us that 'tomorrow we will run faster' to reach the green light, the eternal illusion. But like Gatsby, we will never reach it, and if we attempt to, destruction will surely follow." All you need to do in your ending sentence is summarize the main idea of your essay and add a new viewpoint or thought to bring it full circle.

Feel confident in writing all your essay answers. It's easy and effortless when you use this four-step process: Budget time, outline, write, and proofread.

TAKEAWAYS

- Ace True/False and Multiple-Choice Tests
- Budget Your Time Before You Start Working on Objective Tests
- Answer Essay Questions with Confidence
- Learn a Highly Efficient Outlining System
- Use Your Own Abbreviations in Your Outline
- Write Your Essay Using Your Outline
- Leave Time to Proofread Your Essay

DISCUSS

- Which type of test do you consider most challenging, objective or multiple-choice tests?
- Explain a good technique for approaching objective (true/false and multiple-choice) tests.
- Discuss this book's system for answering essay questions. How can you put this system into action?
- Why is proofreading an important part of perfecting your essays? How much time should you devote to it in a testing situation?
- Discuss how using shortcuts in your essay outline can help you write an excellent essay answer.

Chapter 9

Choose a Major in Line with Your Passion

TALK TO PEOPLE IN YOUR CHOSEN CAREER

In your sophomore or junior year of college, you'll have to choose a major. You can always change it as your decision isn't carved in stone. However, if you do, you may lose credits, have to take additional courses, and need to play catch up. Since it's a big decision with many ramifications, start thinking about what you choose to major in early in your college years.

If, after a while, you believe you've chosen the wrong major, your advisor can possibly arrange for you to count some of the required courses you've taken as electives so that you won't have to take a lot of extra courses. The earlier you decide on a major the better, and the earlier you decide that you want to change it, you'll have more options without the hassle of taking too many extra classes.

Some well-meaning friends and family members may advise you to err on the side of practicality and to choose a major that will give you the most money and prestige. Instead, consider the option of choosing a major you love, one that will bring you joy for the rest of your life. That means following your passion by deciding on a major and career that involves doing something you love, something that excites and inspires you. That said, it's also important to choose a major that will help you find a job to give you a good salary and benefits.

Sophia, a sophomore in a big city university, was confused about her choice of a major. She decided to major in math in the college of liberal arts because she loved dealing with numbers and wanted to make a career of it; however, she wasn't sure about which career path she'd choose.

Sophia mentioned that one of her main interests was dabbling in the stock market and tracking its ups and downs to get the most out of her money. She talked to her advisor about it, and he told her he knew some math majors who had minor areas of study in the stock market.

When she expressed interest in this idea, he told her to take as many courses as she could related to stocks and bonds and to emphasize that on her résumé when she applied for a job. She also needed to showcase her liberal arts degree as an asset so that future employers would see it that way. Additionally, she decided to emphasize her special interest in the stock market to increase her desirability to employers in that field. Sophia loved the stock market and wanted to eventually help others invest their money successfully as she did.

Therefore, she chose math for a major and finance as a minor because math was her first love, and finance, mainly the stock market, was a close second. She ultimately landed a profitable job with an investment company.

Sophia's liberal arts math degree and her minor in finance had served her well. She also spent time writing a killer résumé that highlighted the advantages of her liberal arts degree and her confidence in becoming an excellent financial advisor who had both the academic background and people skills to make money for the company and herself.

CONSIDER ADDING A MINOR THAT OFFERS JOB OPPORTUNITIES

Consider choosing a minor, as Sophia did, that will supplement or enhance your employability. Many education majors, both elementary and secondary, say that choosing a minor greatly enhanced their chances for employment when they applied for jobs.

Some of these students, both prospective elementary and high school teachers, opted for a special education minor, which gave them more options when they applied for a job. One student, Verity, who wanted to work in a school that offered English as a Second Language, took Spanish as a minor, so that she could communicate better with all her students and also expand her job options in case she decided not to teach.

Many venues on the internet give statistics about job opportunities and salaries they offer, along with rankings of the best-paying jobs and types of jobs you qualify for with different degrees. They also tell you if the jobs you seek require advanced degrees. You can't be one hundred percent sure that you've picked the right major and minor, but it's wise to start thinking about it in your freshman year and to begin talking to people working in the fields that most interest you.

Here's what one college junior decided about choosing a minor. Jackson's college advisor thought he should choose a minor since English education was a major that offered minimal teaching jobs on the high school level. Jackson decided to take her advice and add a French minor to his English education major. He loved the language and the culture and knew that job opportunities were plentiful in that subject. It's interesting to note that Jackson chose English education as a major, instead of liberal arts English so that his program would help him obtain teacher certification in a more timely manner. If he'd started out majoring in liberal arts English, he would have to take extra courses to certify him to teach.

When you consider adding a minor, think about how it can help make you more employable and check out job statistics in that area. In Jackson's case, adding the French minor required a few more credits and passing a Modern Language Association proficiency exam with written and oral components in order to qualify for a teaching certificate.

In every case, students like Sophia and Jackson were glad they'd chosen a minor, even if it meant adding a few additional credits to their course load. Another one of these students, Carlos, added health and fitness as a minor to his physical education major since he dreamed of opening a gym one day.

RESEARCH PROS AND CONS OF A JOB IN YOUR FIELD

You may love history and the thought of being a history major (pick your subject), but the thought of disciplining students in a classroom setting and dealing with irate parents may send shivers down your spine. Carefully study the pros and cons of each career you consider, along with having honest conversations with people who work in jobs related to the major.

Matisse, a young man in a religious-affiliated university's student teaching program, dreamed all his life of becoming a teacher because one of his high school teachers had taken him under his wing and inspired him to love learning. He was at the stage where he'd completed all his courses, and the only requirement left for him to complete was to sign up for student teaching. He thought he'd find it rewarding because he loved history, his major, and he looked forward to teaching teenagers.

As the term progressed, he discovered that nothing had prepared him to deal with the grind of discipline. When he found out he'd teach advanced classes in a high school, he never thought he'd have to deal with serious behavior problems, and nothing he did to control his classes seemed to work. He remembered that one of his teachers flicked the lights on and off to restore order when things in his classroom got out of hand, so he used that technique whenever he lost control of the class. His university supervisor mentioned that if something didn't work, he needed to stop doing it and try another technique, but he couldn't get past turning the lights off and on.

None of Matisse's teacher mentors or teachers he knew from high school had ever confided in him about the frustration of having one student disrupt an entire class, making it impossible for others to learn. Even his mentor from his high school who'd encouraged him to become a teacher did not address the feeling of futility he'd felt when an administrator told him that he may not be cut out for teaching. Matisse thought that his teacher/friend felt embarrassed for him and didn't know how to react.

Matisse also had a couple of parents complain that he was too easy on the kids and that he didn't know how to stand up to them. He was also frustrated by having to go by the book to prepare his lessons in accordance with the prescribed curriculum guidelines. He wanted to teach in a more innovative, creative way, using debates and reenacting historic events, as his mentor had instructed him in the alternative school he'd attended.

In the academic high school where Matisse did his student teaching, if a student teacher (or regular one, for that matter), deviated from the course of study, the department head or assistant principal would reprimand them. The cooperating teacher from the school and the university supervisor could both rate the teacher unsatisfactory for not going by the book.

Matisse plodded on, enough to earn a *C* in student teaching, an eight-credit course. He knew that he'd never get a job with a mediocre grade like that for his practice teaching experience, but by then it was too late. Even though Matisse taught two advanced placement classes during student teaching, he faced challenges from his students and found his experience frustrating and unrewarding, not at all what he'd expected.

After he'd spent four years in college studying history education, he decided he didn't want to teach high school history. If he'd talked more to his mentor and other teachers he knew, he may have gotten more insights about the reality of the job. He learned the hard way during student teaching that teaching wasn't what he'd envisioned: getting up in front of a class and discussing current events and having an animated but peaceful give-and-take with the class.

The reality was that in every class a teacher would probably have at least one, maybe more, students who would challenge them or disrupt their class. If a student teacher didn't know how to deal with behavior problems on a daily basis, maybe they wouldn't be a good candidate for a teaching job.

When Matisse and his college advisor talked, she suggested some alternatives to working in a high school setting, and they agreed that while he loved the subject matter, he didn't enjoy the daily frustrations of the job. He decided to get a job as a retail manager since he'd worked in retail all through high school and enjoyed dealing with customers.

He'd also go to grad school part time to prepare him for a job as a history professor in a community college, where discipline probably wouldn't pose as much of a problem. If he couldn't find a job right away, he'd be okay with working in his retail job as he found it much less stressful than working in a high school, even with the boss hovering over him and customers' complaints.

Lauren, a college junior who majored in business, told her advisor she loved working in an office as a summer job, but eventually the routine and tedium of the job and the sense of sitting in her little cubby all day made her crave a job in which she'd interact more with people throughout the day. She knew that being an office manager would not suit her well as her career.

She decided to change her major from business to social work in her junior year. Luckily, she had to attend classes only one additional semester. Her advisor helped her sign up for school courses in three summer sessions to make up for the credits she lacked for the social work program, and she was able to graduate with her class.

THINK ABOUT IT LONG AND HARD

When it's time for you to choose a major, spend time considering whether you'd love to do the job as your life's work. Talk to the people you know who have worked in the job for a few years. Ask them to level with you about the good parts of their job and also the problems and pitfalls. Find out if they had it to do over whether they'd choose the same career path.

Ask them about opportunities for advancement in the job and what kind of training that entails. Find out what they like best about the job and what they find daunting. Ask about salaries and benefits and see if they're in line with the kind of lifestyle to which you aspire. Then make your decision based on your own feelings about your prospective career and their honest assessment of it.

In line with this, Morris, a colleague, related the story of Jake, a sea-soned veteran of the high school classroom who came to his job every day with a morose, hangdog face. On more than a few occasions when Jake signed in for work, he'd say in a flat affect, "I hate this place." Morris wondered how anyone could dislike a job so strongly and remain in it. As it turned out, Jake stayed on the job until his retirement, making himself miserable.

Jake hid his discontent from his students and the administration and earned a satisfactory rating in his evaluations, but his heart wasn't in it. He didn't have a chance to enjoy his retirement because he acquired a serious illness shortly after he left. Some of his colleagues speculated that it may be have been caused by the pent-up stress from hating his job that he experienced over the course of thirty-five years. If you don't love what you do, it may affect you for years to come, even after you're no longer working.

CONSIDER YOUR EARNING POTENTIAL

In addition to your love for the subject matter you choose for your major, think about your earning potential and how much you think you'll need to meet the expenses for the lifestyle you desire. Consider the job prospects for your chosen career in relation to both factors. When Melissa, a lifelong friend, got to the point of choosing a college major, she decided to major in broadcasting because she thought it would be exciting to be a TV newscaster.

However, she found out from friends who'd majored in broadcasting that there weren't many job openings for women at the time in that field, so she thought about how much she'd always enjoyed teaching and loved writing and literature. Melissa spoke to a few teachers in the field and they told her truthfully what they dealt with on a daily basis, both the joys and difficulties of the job. She thought it may be a challenge, but she felt she could handle it.

A couple of her teacher friends invited her to sit in on some of their classes, and when she did, she marveled at how easily they got their classes to comply with their directions. Class control was a breeze for them. Would it be for her? She'd seen some of her own teachers struggle with this aspect of the job, and some even quit before they'd put in a couple of years.

She decided to give it a try, especially since she and her husband-to-be were just starting out and needed jobs that provided a steady income.

As it turned out, Melissa reported that her teaching job was fun although challenging at times. She enjoyed every moment of it. She was glad she went into the profession knowing what to expect. Only people working in the field could have given her that valuable advantage.

ADD A MINOR THAT OFFERS
JOB OPPORTUNITIES

Shayna, a junior in a state university, added a couple of writing courses to her social work degree (without making English a minor) as she'd learned that the job requires writing reports about clients. Later, she said that the grammar/writing courses helped her in her job by giving her a good grasp of the written word.

If you don't want to add a minor to your major, consider taking a couple of courses in the summer or between semesters that will add to your credentials when you apply for jobs. For example, a medical student who plans to work in a community where people mainly speak a language other than English may want to take basic college courses in that language or take online courses to enhance their ability to better serve their clientele.

When you choose a college major, look into adding a minor or an extra course that will boost your résumé and enhance your earning potential during your career. You'll follow your passion by choosing the major that appeals to you most while ensuring your financial future.

TAKEAWAYS

- Discuss Future Careers with Those Who Have Worked in Them
- Consider Adding a Minor to Enhance Job Prospects
- Research Pros and Cons of Careers You're Considering
- Think about Your Earning Potential for Careers that Interest You
- Strive for Job Satisfaction and Earning Potential in Jobs That Appeal to You

DISCUSS

- Why is it helpful to discuss your future career options with someone who has worked in that field?
- What careers are you considering, and who do you know who can advise you about them?
- How can it help you to have a minor in addition to your major? Relate this specifically to a career you're thinking of entering.
- Do you believe it's possible to find both job satisfaction and good earning potential in a future career? If so, discuss someone you know who has found both of these positive traits in the job they chose.

Chapter 10

Plan for the Future

CHOOSE A PATH THAT'S RIGHT FOR YOU

Once you have a couple of years of college under your belt and have committed to a major, and hopefully, a minor that will increase your job prospects, you'll gain confidence in making your decisions going forward. It's never too early to look ahead to what you're going to do after you graduate as decisions you make now may impact your future career plans.

Because the economy fluctuates and is filled with uncertainty, especially when it comes to certain jobs, be sure you plan your curriculum in the best possible way from the beginning to heighten future employment opportunities. At the same time, remember that it's important to love what you do because you'll work in your job for a long time. It's also beneficial to prepare for a job that will give you many different options so you can qualify for a variety of positions within your field, change positions within the same company, or move to another company if it provides better opportunities.

CHOOSE AMONG MANY PATHS

After you graduate, you can look for a job immediately, begin graduate school in your major or another field, or apply to a professional school, such as a medical, dental, or law school. Finding a job immediately after graduation can prove more difficult than many students think. Your search for a job will become harder if you have a major that doesn't lend itself to immediate employment, such as liberal arts, English, psychology, history, or biology. That's not to say it's not possible to find a job in these areas, particularly if you have work/study experience or your résumé stands out as few others do.

Aiden, an English major at a large urban university in New York, is a young person who took a different path than the one he'd originally thought he would. He carried a heavy course load and earned a 4.0 average all four years. He wanted to attend law school after college, and his advisor agreed that an English liberal arts major would prepare him well because it would hone his speaking and writing skills, two necessary requirements for succeeding in the legal field.

Since he'd worked hard for his undergrad degree, he felt emotionally exhausted at the end of his undergraduate years, and decided, instead of applying to law school, to look for a job. He'd also failed to save enough money to get him through a first semester of law school, even if he did get accepted.

Aiden discovered that the only jobs he qualified for in his home town were editorial assistant for a small publisher, local newspaper reporter, or library assistant. To his dismay, these jobs barely covered the rent in the efficiency apartment he lived in with his college friend. He'd heard from a friend that a local sports bar paid well and offered flexible hours if he chose to attend grad school part-time. He landed the bartending job right after applying and got along well with the boss from the start.

However, Aiden missed the give and take about literature and writing in his classes and felt that there was a gaping hole in his life since he started bartending. Would he be able to get that feeling of job satisfaction back again, or would he be stuck forever in a dead-end job? Would he eventually find employment in a field where he'd do well financially that would bring him the satisfaction that he thought practicing law would?

Aiden decided that the only way he'd achieve his dream of attending law school was if he scrimped and saved for a couple of years by working as a bartender, a job that was bearable, but offered little intellectual stimulation. He also decided to make the job more fun by interacting more with his customers and getting them to tell their own unique stories as he mixed drinks and offered bowls of snacks at the bar.

Eventually, the job became less of a chore and more enjoyable, enough to inspire him to write a short piece for a major publication about the joys and pitfalls of tending bar. He also landed an interview with a local radio station, which led to more invitations to write articles and a series in a prestigious national magazine about college graduates finding jobs after graduation that were completely unrelated to their areas of study.

Besides earning extra money from these gigs and feeding his desire to write and speak publicly, Aiden gained confidence in his ability to identify and achieve what he wanted to do for the rest of his life: study law and practice it. Because of his stellar academic record and the notoriety he gained from his writing jobs, the law school of his choice accepted him, and now he's on his way to becoming a practicing attorney. His experience working in the bar will serve him well, and he learned important life lessons from his time spent on the job.

DO YOU WANT TO GO STRAIGHT TO GRADUATE SCHOOL?

Instead of searching for a job immediately after graduation, some students decide to continue their studies by applying to graduate school. They believe that going to graduate school will enhance their chances of getting a better job, but in some cases, these dreams don't materialize. Be sure to research how much a graduate degree will factor into your employability in the area in which you're seeking a job.

As noted in the segment about jobs in the educational field, gaining a graduate degree immediately after leaving undergrad school may work against you since many school districts do not want to pay the extra money that usually goes with an advanced degree. In cases like this, you're better off working and going part-time to graduate school so that after you're working in the field for a while, you can command a higher salary.

Conversely, with some career options, like health care administration, computer science, and marketing, if you're looking for a management position, it may help you to attend graduate school before entering the job market. Take time to research job requirement statistics before you make your decision.

WORK WHILE PLANNING FOR THE FUTURE

Lily, a graduate student, worked as a restaurant server for the past year. She'd graduated from the school of journalism in a small suburban college campus with a 3.0 average and also worked part-time covering political meetings for a local newspaper near her college. Although the editor there recommended her highly for her dream job, writing feature articles for a well-regarded metropolitan daily newspaper close to her home, the management awarded the job to someone who had a year's experience writing for a suburban paper.

Around this time, her friend Marley told her about a family restaurant that was seeking servers. She'd been working there since graduating from college two years ago with a psychology degree and found herself in the same position as Lily of not finding a job in her field. The restaurant paid well, and she made a lot of extra cash in tips.

Lily's friend decided to continue working at the restaurant and to attend grad school part-time to earn a master's in organizational psychology to prepare her for a career as a director of training or director of human resources, two careers that appealed to her. To save money and time commuting, she decided to attend an online school that had high recommendations.

Lily liked the idea of going to grad school part-time so that she could continue earning money in her lucrative server's job in the restaurant where her friend worked. She wanted to continue living in the apartment she rented with her cousin and not be forced to move back to her parents' home, where she'd have to live in her cramped childhood room, sharing a bathroom with her brother and parents.

She dreamed of finding a job for a big city newspaper writing about environmental issues, so she decided to get a master's in environmental science by going part-time to a large university near her home. Possibly, she could also write articles for national publications about environmental issues, such as clean air and water.

Now she believes that her waitress job is helping her in her goal of working as an environmental journalist. She's taking six credits a semester, and although it will take her time to reach her goal, she's staying with her plan because she believes she'll ultimately receive opportunities in her chosen field.

If she doesn't find her dream job, she'll remain flexible and work part-time for the local newspaper until a permanent opening, especially one that deals with environmental issues, comes up. Lily feels proud that she's written a few op-ed pieces for her local paper about environmental problems surfacing in the area and what the local and state governments were doing to address them.

The editor at the newspaper was pleased with her work and offered her part-time work covering local school board and political meetings in the evenings after her waitress shift ended for the day. The work was not to her liking, and the meetings often lasted late into the night, but she considered it a stepping stone to better assignments, which she eventually obtained. She hoped that the newspaper would eventually offer her a full-time job once she completed her master's requirements.

CONSIDER A FELLOWSHIP

Another option after graduation is to apply for a fellowship if that will help you find a job in the career you're seeking. Fellowships often come with funding from the government or the organizations that sponsor them. If you want to do research in your chosen field or teach in a university, a fellowship may be right for you. You won't have to pay taxes on your fellowship if you're a United States citizen. Getting a fellowship will also help you advance into a leadership position in a college or business. Be forewarned: Getting a fellowship is highly competitive; those offering them only accept students who have the best qualifications, and they monitor candidates closely.

It helps, at least in general terms, to consider postgraduate plans so that you have a road map of where you want to end up. Everything you do should lead to a plan that you'll implement upon graduation. If you need to revise it, that's not a problem. With your advisor's help you can do it.

WRITE A WINNING RÉSUMÉ

Whether you plan to find a job after graduation or apply to graduate school or a fellowship, pay particular attention to writing your résumé and to sharpening your oral interview skills in order to secure a job, a position in graduate school, or a coveted fellowship. Make your résumé one page. Highlight your academic career and any volunteer work or relevant jobs you've held while going to college. List awards and honors you've received and any extracurricular activities in which you've participated.

Don't worry about sounding like a braggart. This is the time for you to strut your stuff and shine. Employers and college personnel expect you to showcase your attributes to the fullest in order to get a clear picture of the assets you'd bring to the job, graduate school, or fellowship.

Organize your résumé in bullet form so that those reading can tell at a glance exactly who you are and why you deserve what you're seeking. Be sure to list all items in order of priority.

Choose people with strong credentials in your field for your references, people you can trust to give you the best recommendation possible.

COME OUT ON TOP IN ORAL INTERVIEWS

In order to stand out in oral interviews, dress the part. In interviews for jobs, grad school, and fellowships, show off your best appearance. Add red to the mix, even if it's only a scarf or a necktie, because it's a high-power color and draws people to you like a magnet.

Do you know that part at the end of most interviews where the interviewer asks if you have any questions? Be sure to respond to this one. It can help you get the job. Many people seeking jobs have used this reply to their advantage.

Dr. Monica Uhlhorn, a former superintendent of schools, offers this suggestion that works like a charm. Some students call it "the secret sauce" for a perfect interview. At the conclusion of the interview, when the interviewer asks if you have any questions, say this: "Yes, I have one. What qualities do you look for in your ideal (employee, student, or fellowship) applicant?"

When the people conducting the interview name the quality or qualities they consider important, respond that you've demonstrated that quality or qualities they've mentioned. Explain briefly exactly how you showed that characteristic in previous jobs or in your life experience.

By giving this answer, you're using their ideas as a starting point and building upon them with your answer. You're stating exactly how you'll be the best person to choose for the job. This is a win-win situation for you as you're reinforcing their thoughts and accepting them and also stating how you will go about making their vision for an ideal candidate a reality.

Address the qualities that each interviewer lists and explain how you can demonstrate them. Say something like this after they say what they're looking for in their ideal candidate: "I believe I'm your ideal candidate because . . ." Then list how you've demonstrated the qualities they mentioned. Remember to answer the question directly, clearly, and concisely with sincerity and enthusiasm.

How you speak is as important as what you say. During your interview use the best wording you can muster with strict attention to grammar. Speak loudly enough for everyone to hear you well and with expression. Avoid verbal tics like "ah" and "um" and whatever your own personal bloopers are. Also, add eye contact to your best advantage and look at each person individually when you address them.

TAKEAWAYS

- Think about a Career Path Now
- Plan your Curriculum with an Eye on the Future
- Consider Your Choices (job, grad or professional school, or fellowship)
- It's Never too Early to Think About Future Plans
- Write a Winning Résumé
- Come out on Top in Interviews
- The Secret Sauce for a Perfect Interview

DISCUSS

- What kinds of career options are open to you after college besides applying for a job immediately after you graduate?
- Which tips in this book are most helpful to you in writing a job résumé?

- What are some important things to remember to help you succeed in oral job interviews?
- If you've ever gone on a job interview, what was the most difficult part of the interview for you? If you listed one, how would you approach the next interview you take differently?
- Explain the book's idea of The Secret Sauce for a perfect interview. How do you think it would work for you when you apply for a job?

Chapter 11

Questions and Answers about College

QUESTIONS FOR PARENTS AND INCOMING STUDENTS TO ASK WHEN TOURING A COLLEGE

In addition to considering these questions, be sure to ask about any of your major concerns at the outset rather than wait until a problem comes up. The admissions department is happy to help answer all your questions.

1. Explain how the security process works on your campus and what I need to pay attention to most to stay safe.
2. What kind of experiences or opportunities do you have for new freshmen coming to your school?
3. To what extent is the faculty willing to help if a student is struggling in class? What opportunities do you offer to help students who face trouble with a subject?
4. What kinds of tutoring programs do you offer?
5. What counseling services does your college offer students? Explain the different services of the counseling department. When should students call on the counseling services to help them, and what is the procedure?
6. What is the average class size of introductory classes?
7. What is the average class size of students in my major?
8. What transportation services are available if a student wants to go home for a weekend?
9. What are the advantages of a rural versus a city campus?

10. What is social life like on your campus?
11. Is it hard to meet people if I'm not in a fraternity or sorority? If you don't want to be in one, what's the best way to meet people? Can I still feel connected to the school if I don't join a fraternity or sorority?
12. What are crime statistics for your campus? What types of crimes are the most frequent?
13. What is the political leaning of most of your students? How does it factor in to how a student gets along with faculty and fellow students here?
14. What role, if any, does the college play in controlling students' behavior outside of class?
15. What is your drug and alcohol policy?
16. How important are sports in your college? What priority does the university place on them? What other extracurricular activities besides sports do you offer students?

QUESTIONS FROM KIDS ABOUT COLLEGE

Question: My professor gets on my nerves, and I want to drop his class. He talks in a monotone and gives impossible tests. I need the course to graduate, and there are only two teachers who teach this class, including mine. Should I try to switch teachers? I've heard that teachers in the same department know one another and sometimes talk about their students. I don't want to cause trouble for myself.

Answer: If it's mainly a personality conflict, try to stick with the course. If you think you won't have a chance to do well in the class, you may want to talk it over with your advisor or a peer counselor to get their take on it. If you need the class and believe you can overlook your professor's foibles enough to succeed, try to overlook them. However, if you consider how the professor operates a deal breaker, think about making a move. The decision is up to you.

Question: What is some good advice you can give me about pacing myself in college so I don't get overwhelmed or burned out?

Answer: Take good care of your mental health. In college there's so much to do at once, plus pressure to get good grades. It's okay to slow down and not to take too many courses in a semester. Spend time with friends and forge an identity outside of being a student.

Question: If I have some latitude in choosing my teachers, what should I look for?

Answer: Choose teachers who are knowledgeable, but who also show empathy and kindness. The best way to gain this information about them is by word of mouth from other students who have taken these teachers' classes. Sometimes, you don't have a choice, especially in the first year, so you have to learn to adjust to the professors to which you're assigned and make the best of it.

Question: My roommate is being super rude. How do I ask him to stop or get out of this room arrangement?

Answer: Talk to him and tell him exactly how you feel about how he's acting toward you. If you don't see any change, go to your resident advisor and see what they say, or ask for a meeting between you, your roommate, and the resident advisor. You should be able to get your problem resolved without going higher. If you don't, see a student ombudsman or ask a key person in the Dean of Students' office who to contact about a room change. If you're fearful of your roommate's behavior toward you, don't hesitate to consult the student safety or security department.

Question: What are the most important things I should know when I meet with my academic advisor?

Answer: Be sure to get everything your advisor tells you about course requirements in writing, so if they leave, you'll have some protection. Sometimes, advisors make mistakes about which courses you need. If you're concerned about something they tell you not being the best information, verify it in the Dean of Students' office.

Question: What's the best way to find out what each of my professors expect of me?

Answer: Pay close attention during the first week of class to what your professors tell you about their course requirements and what you can expect regarding the types, frequency, and content of tests. Also, see how your teachers' body language reinforces their message. Ask your professors questions regarding things you need clarified about the subject matter when exam time rolls around.

Question: What can I do to make my college adjustment easier?

Answer: When you go to orientation and during the first weeks of classes, make friends. You'll find them in the lounge, the dining hall, and in your dorm complex. Find a network of friends that you can bounce things off of and trust. Reciprocate by being a good and reliable friend and listener. If you have problems adjusting to college life, don't hesitate to find a peer counselor or visit the counseling center. You'll find many people willing to help you.

Question: I'm thinking about joining a sorority but I don't know if it's for me. How can I tell if I should go out for one? I'm somewhat leery of rushing one because if I'm not accepted as a pledge I'll feel bad, and I don't deal well with rejection.

Answer: Do you like mainly hanging out with the same group or do you prefer having friends from different ones? If you're in a sorority or fraternity, it's likely you'll spend a lot of your time with your sorority sisters or brothers. If that's okay with you, you'll be fine joining one. If you like having friends from a lot of different social circles, then you may be better off not joining one. It's your choice. If you apply and aren't accepted by a sorority, you'll still have many opportunities to find a lot of friends on campus.

Question: What's the best way to stay healthy as a college student?

Answer: Whether you're a commuter or a dorm resident, college life can have an impact on your physical and emotional well-being. For one thing, you'll have a full schedule and will have to get used to the stress of studying for exams and making the grades you want. Also, you'll have to get used to your new surroundings, new friends, and teachers who may use a different approach from your high school teachers. In order to maintain good physical and psychological health, it's important to budget your time and make time to do things you like with people whose company you enjoy. You'll also want to give attention to eating healthy foods and staying away from junk food, although it won't hurt to indulge yourself with a favorite snack or dessert every so often. It's also crucial to find a type of exercise you like because if you don't like it, you'll either do it grudgingly or won't do it at all. Finally, leave time for some type of regular relaxation, like meditation, yoga, or walking.

Question: What are the implications of choosing a college major for your future job?

Answer: As stated throughout this book, it's important to choose a major that goes along with the kind of work you'd most enjoy doing throughout your life. Think of all the different jobs for which you could qualify by choosing this major. If the major doesn't offer many different job possibilities, you may want to rethink your choice before committing to a major that won't give you different employment options. If you're interested in two areas of study, you may want to choose a double major or a minor along with your major (see next question for information about minors). Above all, it's important that you love the area that you choose to study because you'll be working in this area for many years.

Question: My advisor tells me that I should choose a minor in addition to a major. Why is that important? I'm only interested in teaching elementary kids, and there's no other subject I like.

Answer: If you choose a minor, it will enhance your job possibilities. For example, if you're an education major, you may want to choose special education or a language taught in schools, such as Spanish, as a minor so you'll have opportunities to find jobs that call for more flexibility in subject matter. If you're a liberal arts major, look into secondary teaching certification as part of your program so that you're qualified to teach middle school and high school as well as college. Similarly, if you're a business major, you can choose a language as a minor and qualify for jobs in international business.

Question: Suppose I don't like my major after trying it out for a while? Should I change it or stick with it?

Answer: Most students don't believe it's wise to stay in a major they don't enjoy. It's important to love what you study and ultimately choose for your life's work. If you do change it, work with your advisor to see if you can fit some of the courses you've taken already into a new major as electives. If you can't do that, be prepared to lose some credits that are unrelated to your new major.

In the end, it may be worth changing your major because staying in one you don't like won't work to your advantage now or when you look for a job. The most important asset you can display in an interview is your enthusiasm for a job you're seeking. Without that passion for the subject matter, it's hard to fake that.

Remember this above all else: You can and will succeed if you have the inspiration and the motivation. You can solve any problems that come up by relying on your own common sense and all the resources your college offers. Go for it!

About the Author

Catherine DePino wrote twenty books about bullying, grammar/writing, spirituality, and women's issues. She recently published *How to Ask for and Get What You Want* and *Parenting Mindfully: 101 Ways to Help Raise Caring and Responsible Kids in an Unpredictable World.* Her self-help book, *Fire Up Your Life in Retirement: 101 Ways for Women to Reinvent Themselves*, helps women deal with the challenges they face in retirement. Her bully prevention book, *Blue Cheese Breath and Stinky Feet: How to Deal with Bullies* (APA), was published in many different languages. Bully prevention programs value it as a treasured resource. She also wrote *Helping Kids Live Mindfully: A Grab Bag of Activities for Middle School Students.*

Her background includes a BS in English and Spanish education, a master's in English education, and a doctorate in Curriculum Theory and Development and Educational Administration with principal's certification, all from Temple University.

The author worked for thirty-one years as a teacher, department head, and disciplinarian in the Philadelphia School District. After this, she worked at Temple as an adjunct assistant professor and student teaching supervisor.

Catherine has also written articles for national magazines, including *The Christian Science Monitor*, and *The Writer.* She views her most important accomplishment in life as being the mother of three children and the grandmother of five.

For many years, she served on the board of The Philadelphia Writers' Conference and has acted as a manuscript judge and speaker. Visit her website at www.catherinedepino.com.